Turkish Cooking

Turkish Cooking

A Culinary Journey through Turkey

Text and Illustrations by
Carol Robertson

Photographs by
David Robertson

Frog, Ltd.
Berkeley, California

Turkish Cooking
A Culinary Journey through Turkey

Published by Frog, Ltd.

Frog, Ltd. books are distributed by
North Atlantic Books
P.O. Box 12327
Berkeley, California 94712

Cover and book design by Paula Morrison
Typeset by Catherine Campaigne

Printed in the United States of America

Distributed to the book trade by Publishers Group West

Library of Congress Cataloging-in-Publication Data

Robertson, Carol, 1942–
    Turkish cooking : a culinary journey through Turkey / Carol Robertson.
        p.   cm
    Includes index.
    ISBN 1-883319-38-2 (hc)
    1. Cookery, Turkish.   2. Turkey—Description and travel.
3. Turkey—Social life and customs.   I. Title.
TX725.T8R627   1996
641.59561—dc20   95-18912
                                                          CIP

        1 2 3 4 5 6 7 8 9 / 00 99 98 97 96

This book is dedicated to the members of our family who have patiently endured our travel tales and photos over the years . . . Jennifer, Erica, Jim G., Marie, Subagh S., Subagh K., Simran, Jim R., Betty, Heather, and Jackie . . .

. . . with a special thanks to Erica Robertson and Lee Roby for their many helpful suggestions, Robert Kayser of Rochester Institute of Technology for photographic assistance, and David Robertson for long hours of typing and editing.

6/4/96

Table of Contents

Introduction

PLEASE TRAVEL WITH US TO TURKEY. But first, allow us to introduce ourselves: a teacher and an artist, each with a self-avowed passion and desire to see the world. The earth and man's marks upon it are often so astounding and wonderful that we constantly seem to be planning our next journey.

We've traveled over many lands and continents, often returning two and three times to some area that we regard with special affection, to delve deeper into the land, people, arts, architecture, and cuisine. Turkey is one country that we hold in particular esteem and have chosen to return to. In truth, we have seldom found a place that manages to combine such an incredible layering of history—truly a crossroads—with warm and engaging people, physical beauty of all kinds, and one of the great cuisines of the world.

So journey with us to this magical land. Perhaps you have never been there except in your imagination, and you harbor a desire to go. Perhaps you have been on a whirlwind tour of the "if it's Tuesday it must be Istanbul" variety. Or perhaps you have been lucky enough to have the time to explore the land in all its complexity. It is a country for history buffs, those who appreciate fine arts and crafts, and lovers of good food. If you have been there, you will certainly remember a beautiful landscape, fascinating reminders of history, honest and happy people, beautiful arts and handicrafts, and, most definitely, the food! Every small village café, every sophisticated big city restaurant, every chef and every homemaker is involved in the production of foods so pure and nutritious, so palatable and appealing to modern tastes that it is hard to believe that most of the body of recipes we call Turkish cuisine were standardized centuries ago in the palaces of the Ottoman rulers.

The stories in this book are from our travel journals, the photographs from our cameras, the illustrations from our hands, but the recipes are a pure taste of Turkey.

This small book is meant to be neither a complete guide to travel, nor a complete guide to Turkish cooking. Rather, we have chosen a few places and stories to evoke the feel of the country. It is simply two travelers' accounts of experiences in this fabulous land, and a sampling of its classic cuisine; there are hundreds of places yet to be explored, perhaps by you. More importantly, it would insult the complex and sophisticated body of thousands of recipes from the palace kitchens to suggest that our recipe list is complete. But the ones that were chosen for inclusion are the true classics, the most often prepared, and the foods most likely to be sampled there. A true taste of Turkey can be tried by putting together a menu of recipes taken from several sections of this book.

If we have whetted your curiosity about the country, its beauty, its people, and its foods, we will have succeeded. We hope our enthusiasm is contagious as we once again invite you to use our stories and recipes to travel with us to Turkey.

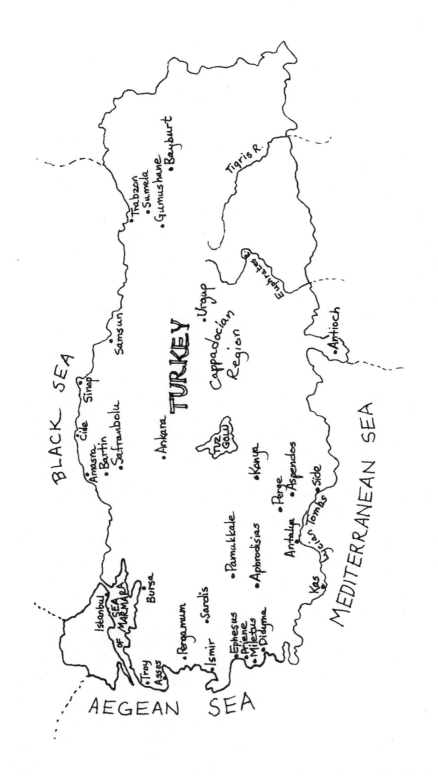

Turkey— The Land and Its History

SOME LANDS ARE DESTINED by geography to play host over the millennia to a great parade of armies, people, and cultures. They are fortunate, however, if there remains behind as evidence of their struggles, a richness of art and architecture, culture, and cuisine. Turkey, the country that occupies the ancient land of Anatolia, is one of the very few places in the world which holds an incredibly complete record of man from his earliest permanent settlements to the great democratic changes of our own century. The cultural wealth of Turkey is astounding, and by visiting there today, one can see the end result of this historical layering.

The land is literally a crossroad between Asia and the Orient, Europe and the Middle East. A cradle of history, a route for trade and for conquest, Turkey is a "land between"; and throughout her history, East and West have alternated in their cultural influence. She has played host to earliest man in the Tigris and Euphrates river valleys, Greek and Roman cities, early Christian and Byzantine cultures, and the Turkoman, Ottoman, and Seljuk empires. Homer, Troy, Constantinople, King Midas, whirling dervishes—these names conjure up colorful images from her past. Many of these cultural groups were wealthy and could support great growth in the arts.

In addition, Anatolia is blessed with a diverse geography. The climate ranges from cool and rainy in the north along the Black Sea, to quite hot most of the year on her southern shores, to bitterly cold in winter in her eastern areas. She has pine forests and snow-capped mountains, miles of beautiful beaches, large lakes, prairies planted in wheat, and deserts. Turkey has a thousand small villages and large sophisticated cites. Ankara is her capital. Istanbul, whose site itself seemed destined to make her a great cultural center, sits astride her East-West gateway. Some of her citizens are nomadic; many more are merchants, farmers, and fisherman. Virtually all are Moslems.

Man's history on the Anatolian peninsula, archaeologists tell us, begins very early indeed with some one million year old human remains recently discovered in a cave near Istanbul. Much later, the valley between the Tigris and Euphrates Rivers, the so called "fertile crescent," holds record of the first towns and cities, and the first permanent farming settlements. These date to 10,000 BC. The ancient people of Anatolia were the first to irrigate fields and probably the first to domesticate animals. The settlements grew in number and population throughout the Bronze Age, leaving their records in pottery and metal. As archaeologists slowly uncover these areas, the fate of each city, such as Troy, can be read.

By 2000 BC, some written documents—clay tablets—help to decipher the past; and by about 1500 BC one group, the Hittites, had become a power to rival the Egyptians. They built massive palaces and forts, and created monumental sculptures. The best of Hittite art is housed in Ankara in the Museum of Anatolian Civilizations, not to be missed for a good understanding of Turkish culture.

By 1000 BC though, the Hittites ceased to exist as a cohesive empire and at about this same time Anatolia began to have new visitors to her western shores. The earliest Greek settlements, principally around Ephesus, were established, and later, major Greek cities were built at Pergamum, Assos, Miletus, and many other sites. Over the next thousand years, spurred on by the conquest of Alexander the Great, the indigenous cultures of Anatolia, such as the Lycians, lost their own languages and arts to the more pervasive Greek culture. Travelers to these areas can see the majestic theaters, temples, and column-lined avenues of Hellenistic Turkey.

Meanwhile, from about 200 BC on, the Romans had been aggressively building their empire to the west of Greece. When they arrived in Anatolia, they wisely kept all that the Greeks had built and added to it. Their columns grew more tall, slender, and ornate; the arch was incorporated into their architectural vocabulary; and their sculpture became more true to life and less idealized. They built arenas, basilicas, and aqueducts, thousands of miles of roads, and hundreds of bridges. The cities of Aphrodisias, Didyma, Side, Ephesus, Pergamum, and others were so added to and embellished by the Romans that it is sometimes difficult to detect the first Greek layer.

Christianity came to Anatolia very early. In the 1st century AD, Saint Paul traveled and preached there, and by the 4th century, there were many churches and monasteries. When the Roman emperor Constantine converted in 312 AD, Christianity was propelled quickly into the state religion. He established Constantinople as the new seat of the religion, and later, in the 6th century, the great basilica of Sancta Sophia was constructed. This is called the Byzantine period. Its art, often in the form of magnificent mosaics, its distinctive architecture, and its literature are explicitly Christian.

By 650 AD, however, the first armies of Islam were already invading Anatolia. The Byzantines lost much of eastern Anatolia to them. The Byzantine empire struggled on for hundreds of years; its fortunes waxing and waning through a final split with Rome, battles with tribesmen in the north, new invasions of Seljuk Turks to the west, and the pressure of foreign Crusader armies. The city of Constantinople was a last holdout in the steadily shrinking empire. Finally, in 1453, it fell to the Ottoman Turks and was quickly renamed Islamboul or City of Islam.

In truth, the art and architecture of much of Anatolia had been slowly changing over the centuries from the Greco-Roman and then Byzantine motifs to ones that could be called Asian. Forms and conventions such as the absence of human representation, ornately geometric surface decoration, and ceramic tiles were replacing mosaics, columns, and haloed saints. A great era of mosque and palace building had begun. Soaring minarets, elaborate tile work, beautiful calligraphy, intricate stalactite ceilings, and rich use of precious jewels and metals all attested to the great wealth of the Ottoman rulers.

It is these motifs that provide the top layer of arts and architecture that has come to form the look of present day Turkey. Although pagan, Christian, and Islamic motifs are often side by side in cities and countryside, many instances of true "layers" (such as Islamic calligraphy covering Byzantine mosaics in Sancta Sophia) are interesting to detect.

Finally, for Anatolia, one more great swing between East and West was to take place in our own century. World War I saw the total defeat of the already weakened Ottoman Empire and the subsequent establishment of the Republic of Turkey, with Kemal Ataturk as its first president. Under his wise leadership, Turkey began to institute changes that would bring it more into line with western ideas. The Latin alphabet was adopted, the veil for women and the fez for men was discouraged, universal education was begun, and most importantly, a democratic constitution was adopted.

The traveler finds modern day Turkey with one foot firmly planted in each of two traditions. A member of NATO, with a government modeled on that of the United States, it still preserves, displays, and honors its great cultures and traditions from the past.

TRAVELER'S TALES
OF TURKEY

Istanbul—
First Impressions

ONCE, YEARS AGO, we remember coming into New York on a late afternoon flight, circling wide over that magnificent skyline, and marveling as the setting sun turned the skyscrapers golden.

No such dramatic view marked our first impression of Istanbul. Rather, we arrived there late one hot night in July and, with our fellow travelers, formed a steamy crush of airport humanity searching for friends, luggage, and taxis.

An hour later a grumpy cab driver delivered us to a less-than-wonderful hotel, and finally, by two in the morning we could rest. It was only the next day that our love affair with this great historic place began.

The first surprise was a breakfast of bread and olives, cheese, yogurt, honey, and melon—to our palates a good start. Afterwards, armed with our map, we took a walk into the old city to the world-famous Covered Bazaar. It consists of four thousand shops housed in a great rectangle of buildings under a hundred domes. The merchants there sell fine jewelry, hand-woven carpets, antiques, ceramics, and traditional crafts.

Entering the bazaar through one of the many portals, we saw veiled women, backpacking young tourists, children, and old men, all making their way from shop to shop through the labyrinth of streets and passageways. A moment of hesitation or any eye contact alerted shopkeepers who were immediately at one's side, encouraging a second look and perhaps a purchase—of course promising the best price.

We walked and looked at the beautiful displays for an hour; in the end we bought nothing, and emerged somewhat dazed from a different portal onto the relative quiet of the avenue.

A few minutes walk further into the old city, quite near to the great mosques, stood a small hotel with an inviting entrance. On a whim we entered and the genial woman at the desk offered to show us her best room—at half the price of our present room!

The fifth floor penthouse room, the only one on that floor, was of medium size. What made it special was a balcony with doors that ran around two sides. It afforded a wonderful view of all of the old city and the Golden Horn, Topkapi Palace, Sancta Sophia, and the Blue Mosque. A phone call, a taxi ride; the change was made quickly and by early afternoon we were in our new room. We were to stay there many days and return again to our "room with a view" on other visits to Istanbul.

Noticing a small outdoor café nearby serving fresh salads, soups, and kebabs, and being hungry for lunch, we walked back up the avenue and settled at a pleasant umbrella-shaded table. We both decided on lentil soup, shepherd's salad, and a cool, refreshing yogurt drink called ayran.

After lunch, we walked for several streets downhill toward the waterfront. In Istanbul, water is key, lying between and around the three peninsulas of land which make up the old city, the new city, and the eastern suburbs. Ferries, great cruise ships, tankers, and big and small craft of all kinds ply the busy waters of the Golden Horn, the Bosporus, and the Sea of Marmara. The speedy ferries especially, look to be on a collision course with anything in their way.

We were at the center of the city now; its heartbeat was nearly audible. Everywhere vendors with pushcarts sell street food, magazines, and clothing. Office workers, families, and tourists join constantly forming and reforming lines to board the ferries which crisscross the three waterways. A broad avenue runs the length of the waterfront and disappears around the curve of the old city peninsula. Traffic is constant; road crossing is an act of courage. And floating above it all is that magical and famous skyline of the old city. One can see the great domes of the mosques surrounded by their tall slim minarets, the many smaller domes of the Egyptian market, and the walls of Topkapi Palace.

Dominating the old city side of the harbor to the south, and stretching across the Golden Horn to the new city, is a two-level floating bridge called the Galata. All manner of motorized and animal-drawn vehicles, and hundreds of pedestrians and bicycles use the upper level. From stands along the railing, men sell grilled fish and roasted corn, donut-shaped bread called simit stacked onto trays held high above their heads, fresh fruit drinks, and blue and white beads to ward off the "evil eye." On the bottom level, reached by steps at several locations along the expanse, are a line of seafood restaurants. Our plan was to return here for dinner, so we turned our attention to the Egyptian market which lay back across the avenue behind us.

Today, it seemed, was our day to visit markets and there is no livelier one than this, which specializes in spices. They are sold in great quantity and variety, but that is not all. Actually, the Egyptian market sells seeds, beans and dried fruits, plants, apothecary items, meats, and cheeses; everything is a colorful blur of activity. We were captivated by the many sights and smells and wandered about asking too many questions of the ever-smiling and cheerful proprietors. How and with what is this spice used? What is the name of that one?

After an hour of this, it was growing late, and we walked back up the hill, really not very far, to our hotel to rest, shower, and dress for dinner.

Later, on the lower level of the Galata Bridge, we chose one restaurant—we had been told that they were all more or less equally competitive—that had a particularly fresh and inviting display of fish on a small mountain of crushed ice. Eating is done *al fresco,* while watching the harbor and the skyline. In Turkey, one chooses or is given several small meze, or snacks, before the main meal. Our choice was stuffed grape leaves, olives, and some fresh feta cheese. Most of the fare at these simple restaurants consists of grilled or deep-fried catch of the day, accompanied by salad and lots of wonderful bread. We chose deep-fried fillets of a delicious local fish called lufer, a kind of bluefish. Turkish restaurants and food shops tend to be highly specialized. Some restaurants serve only one kind of soup alone. Sweet shops make either custards and taffies, or layered pastries such as baklava. Restaurants will serve only meat or only fish. The earliest and oldest guilds of chefs serving in the great Ottoman palaces such as Topkapi specialized to such a degree that each guild would prepare only soups or only vegetable dishes, sometimes in separate kitchens. These divisions persist to this day.

As the sun set on our first day in Istanbul, we fell into conversation with several English-speaking people at the next table. They suggested that after our meal we should ride a ferry to the eastern suburb of Uskudar and back again to really enjoy an impression of the old city at night. With many domes, minarets, and the palace walls flood lit, it promised to be quite a view.

The boats leave every fifteen minutes, and the one we caught a few hundred feet from the restaurant was not crowded. How beautiful she looked, the Queen of Cities, with her famous skyline, the piece of land that has been a fought over prize through the millennia, the link between east and west and two continents.

The round trip did not take very long, and we were soon trudging back up the hill to our hotel, now quite exhausted. As we fell into bed, the evening call to prayer was just ringing out, first from one, then soon with overlapping chants, from all the minarets. Devout Moslems are called this way to pray five times a day; the melancholy cries of the muezzins add yet another dimension to this city that had captivated us in so short a time.

Spas and Hot Springs— Turkish Style

THERE ARE ABOUT ONE THOUSAND thermal springs scattered throughout western Turkey. We decided to visit just two of them. Our first choice was the spa at Bursa. Setting out by car from Istanbul, we followed the highway eastward around the Sea of Marmara to the small town of Darica. There we took a car ferry across a wide bay, then continued south to our destination. The Ottoman rulers made Bursa their first capital, but its history goes back much farther to Roman and pre-Roman times. Its thermal waters have been enjoyed for over two thousand years; we wanted to try them for ourselves.

Bursa is a lovely city, set against Mount Olympos, and overlooking a broad green valley. Our guidebook suggested that we stay in the nearby suburb of Cekirge where the best hotel spas are located. We chose a room with a large window opening onto the valley and settled in for several days, both to bathe in the therapeutic waters which flowed directly into our hotel and to see Bursa's many sights.

The presence of thermal springs in and around the city created, long ago, a need for an absorbent cotton fabric to dry and wrap in. Today the shops in the market are full of what we, not surprisingly, call Turkish toweling. Robes and towels from Bursa are especially thick, luxurious, and beautiful.

A second industry centered in Bursa since the Ottoman days is silk. Most of the silk produced here is used for weaving magnificent carpets. Our visit to Bursa coincided with a silk fair, and people from outlying areas were bringing in silkworm cocoons to sell.

Bursa is also famous for the manufacture of special knives, for having a lively market in antiques, and for possessing many examples of early Ottoman architecture. Among the culinary delights of the area are especially delicious peaches, and the Iskender kebab which consists of roast lamb laid on flat bread and drenched with tomato sauce, yogurt, and melted butter.

Over the next several days, we visited the Old Ottoman markets and bought two big fluffy bathrobes and some lovely silk scarves, passed on the knives and antiques, tasted the peaches and kebabs, and toured the famous mosques and a Turkish han. Somewhat like a hotel, the han consisted of two stories of offices, rooms, and warehouses surrounding a fountained courtyard. Silk brokers and merchants could buy and sell their valuable merchandise here in the walled and gated compound. On the day of our visit in July, displays in the han could not equal the opulence of five hundred years ago, but seeing the beautiful silk products in their original setting was a treat.

The spa in our hotel consisted of a series of marble-lined rooms on the ground floor. In the largest, we would get our towels and robes each day from an attendant who would then show us to our private soaking and bathing suite. The smallest area there was a changing room, and it had several cots for resting. Next to it was a shower and bathing room supplied with hot and cold water, brushes, soaps, and shampoos. From there, several steps led down to a shallow pool, about eight by ten feet square, into which continuously poured large quantities of warm, mineral-laden spring water from a pipe high on the wall. One could luxuriate in the humid atmosphere for hours. The water is widely believed to be beneficial for all manner of health problems. We can't be sure that it's not all true; we know that we enjoyed our days in Bursa because of all we saw and especially because of those wonderfully relaxing soaks in the spa.

Hundreds of miles south and some days later, we were about to experience our second spa. It could not have been more different from Bursa. This one is called Pamukkale and is considered to be the greatest natural wonder in Turkey. After driving across miles of flat farmland, we could see a lone low mountain in the distance. It appeared to be snow-covered but as we got closer we could see that the top several hundred feet was covered with massive crystalline mineral deposits. Closer still, we could pick out hundreds of people walking through what appeared to be sugar-white terraced rice paddies.

The road led us around the base and up the back of the mountain to the top. There, built around several springs which poured from the ground and flowed under and across the road, are hotels, restaurants, and a museum. The hotel in which we found a room is built partially within the walls of an eleventh century Byzantine castle, and its deep pool is constructed to catch the warm salty spring water before allowing it to continue its cascade over the edge and down the terraced mountain. From the pool one has a panoramic view of the valley far below. Whole families explored the natural wonder; women delicately trying to keep their long skirts dry, and children flopping into the shallow water contained in each terrace. Branches, blades of grass, rocks, everything, is coated white. Stone icicles hang from every edge, and one can hear a gentle murmur as the water flows down from pool to pool.

Soon we joined the others to play in the calcium-rich basins which have been used since Roman times. This is ancient Hierapolis, a spa then as now. Several hours of walking and splashing about, and later swimming in our hotel pool, gave us an appetite. A bit of a distance away, across the treeless mountain top, we could see an outdoor restaurant. Most of the walkways are wet and slick, but we carefully picked our way along. We were rewarded with a typically delicious Turkish meal of assorted meze, stuffed eggplant, and a pilav dish with currants and pine nuts. The sunset was magnificent—a bright orange ball, dropping through a hazy cloudless sky. People remained on the terraces until well after dark.

The ruins of the old Roman city spread back across the top of the mountain, and the next day a visit to them and the museum on the site was in order. We have always marveled at the wealth of beautiful statues, columns, sarcophagi, and other stone artifacts from this period that Turkey possesses. Hierapolis does not disappoint. Room after room in the museum is full of Roman sculpture, and any one piece would be the pride of most American museums. Especially fascinating are the faces of senators and other important people of that era rendered in stone with absolute photographic realism. Every line and wrinkle, every unique physical feature, leaps intact across two thousand years.

Later, we took a swim in another pool, this one built right over the sacred spa of Hierapolis. At its bottom lie fragments of the ancient columns, and swimmers glide around them through the slightly effervescent, clear, warm water. What a unique experience! In point of fact, our visit to Pamukkale, the "Cotton Castle," is, in a land full of wonders, certainly one of the most fascinating and unforgettable.

Greek and Roman Wonders

As early as 1100 BC, the city-states of what is now Greece began to venture past their crowded and sometimes besieged lands, and establish new colonies on the western shores of Anatolia. In the 4th century BC, the conquests of Alexander the Great expedited the spread of the Greek language, style and culture.

Centuries later the Romans sent their armies to Anatolia, successfully annexing the lands into their rapidly expanding empire. They wisely chose to build on what the Greeks had begun. Although somewhat concentrated in the southern and western regions of Turkey, the resulting network of towns, cities, roads, bridges, theaters, and temples are an archaeological treasure trove that can be seen throughout the country. There are dozens upon dozens of Greek and Roman sites for the visitor to explore, most still blissfully uncrowded and uncommercialized. We have been to perhaps fifteen or twenty, always tantalized to see more, but usually running out of days.

This time we had about a week, and decided to concentrate on three of the most well known and complete. Fortunately, they are in close proximity to one another. Basing ourselves in Ismir was not a good choice. It is a big city, with an arc of building-covered hills surrounding a shallow sea—too noisy, too busy, and far too crowded to enjoy. Our first excursion was to ancient Pergamum, a short distance north, and we were happy to be on our way. Located in present day Bergama, Pergamum was a great center of learning, medicine and culture in the ancient world. It was the home of a library to rival Alexandria's (it was in Pergamum that parchment was developed), a medical spa, and, high on a hill, a stunning acropolis.

We started there at the top, and followed helpful signs as we wandered the ancient roads, going from the partially restored temples of Trajan and Athena, to a school for the young of Pergamum, and finally to the great theater. Eighty rows of very steeply banked seats offer an unimpeded view of the stage and the valley. The acoustics are said to be perfect, but a trip to the stage below to test them was too heart-stopping to attempt. We wondered how the audiences of those days ever had the courage to inch their way to their seats. Precipitous theaters notwithstanding, the entire area was breathtaking. We imagined it as it was then, with the sea originally coming all the way across today's valley to the foot of the acropolis. How lovely it must have been to stroll along the beautiful avenues past the pristine temples high above the sea, on the way to the schools, the famous library, or the theater. This wonderful city of the ancient world was, in the 1st and 2nd centuries BC, the richest and most powerful in Turkey.

Later we drove the several miles back down the spiral road from the acropolis, and into the old Turkish quarter. The narrow streets there are lined with shops selling the beautiful blue and red Bergama carpets, hung like exotic laundry along the outside walls. We considered the purchase of one over a noonday meal in a small restaurant. We tried a variety of flaky cheese and meat-filled borek, and thick slabs of fried eggplant with yogurt.

We had time in the afternoon to see the lower town and its huge red brick basilica (the meeting hall of the day). Nearby is a Roman bridge, and over it is the archaeological museum and Asklepion medical facility. The doctors of that era practiced a kind of encouraging psychotherapy, cajoling their patients with promises of a cure if they ran a sacred course, drank from sacred springs, and submitted to a kind of dream analysis. The spring still flows, the vaulted course can still be run, and Sigmund Freud, two thousand years later, offered more clues in the art of analyzing nocturnal adventures.

We find that museums greatly help us to put ourselves in a given time and place. Our last stop was at Pergamum's museum, with gardens and interior rooms full of sculpture and fragments found in and around the upper acropolis and lower town. The museum helps visitors envision these glorious pieces back in the temples on the hill or lining the avenue in the Asklepion.

It took over an hour to get back to Ismir, and we were too tired after dinner for anything more than an evening stroll in our hotel neighborhood. But the next day we were ready to travel to Ephesus, about fifty miles to the south, to see what is considered one of the most famous treasures from antiquity. There, a Hellenistic Greek city, quite glorious in its own right, was later added to and embellished by the Romans. What remains today is mostly from the latter period. Ephesus became the capital of Roman Anatolia, just as Pergamum was the Greek center. We knew there was much to see and started out early. The ruins are astonishingly complete, and it takes many hours to see it all. At Ephesus, as at Pergamum, the sea has retreated. It was a bustling seaport in its day, but today there is no water in sight. What can be seen, though, is a magnificently colonnaded and statue-lined main boulevard leading from the old harbor to the amphitheater. Said to hold 25,000, the view is impressive from the topmost of its sixty-six tiers. Crossing the main boulevard in front of the theater is another beautiful road leading to the right and to the left. At one end we went to see what remains of a school, a stadium, and the gate to the acropolis. In the other direction, at the far edge of a three hundred foot courtyard sits the famous library of Celsus. This remarkable building with two stately stories of fine Corinthian columns, has coffered ceilings and many beautiful statues. One can still see niches for scrolls within the library rooms.

Later that day, we visited many other smaller temples, baths and concert halls along a street that runs north behind the theater. All along the way, visitors stop to inspect mosaic floors, statues, columns and Latin inscriptions. Finally at the head of this street are gates to the walled eastern flank of the city. One is filled with admiration for the Romans and their building skills, their attention to detailed stone work, and the sheer livability of their cities. Even the great cities like Ephesus had a human quality. The Roman passion and zest for the life is evident throughout the site.

Returning to our car hours later, we needed some refreshing. Ephesus is located two miles from the town of Selcuk. We headed to a pleasant outdoor restaurant along the main street there, and had no sooner ordered, when, with great amateur fanfare, a small parade started down the street. But what appeared to be a parade was actually a small boy on a horse, surrounded by a group of enthusiastic men. He was costumed like a king, with a crown and a fur-bordered cape aglitter with sequins. We had seen this before in Istanbul, and knew that this young man was on his way to his circumcision ceremony, a time of great celebration for families and a rite of passage for the boy.

After lunch we drove to another site, this time not Roman, but Christian. Saint John traveled here in the 1st century AD, preaching the Gospel and hoping to establish a church. He brought with him the Virgin Mary, and it is widely believed that she lived out her last days and died in a tranquil house about five miles from Ephesus. We drove there, and walked a wooded path to view the house and a small sacred spring.

Before driving back to Ismir we had time to stop and see the rich collection of sculpture at the Ephesus museum. The pride of the museum is the decidedly un-Greek looking statue of Artemis, and the celebrated Boy on a Dolphin, but their collections also include additional dozens of superb works from Ephesus.

Once again we were too tired when we returned to Ismir to do anything more than eat dinner and take a short stroll, but we rewarded our two days of diligent sightseeing with an outstanding meal. Our hotel recommended a seafood restaurant overlooking the water along the main boulevard. We began with stuffed mussels, olives, and puréed eggplant, enjoyed while sipping raki. Our main course consisted of grilled chunks of swordfish alternating with bay leaves on a skewer, and served over pilav. This was accompanied by a simple salad of chopped cucumber in garlic-flavored yogurt, and cooked green beans in tomato sauce. For dessert we each had a tiny honey-soaked flaky pastry with pistachio nuts, and twin demitasse cups of thick Turkish coffee.

Over dinner we decided to take a few days off before going on to our third Roman city, and visit several beach areas up and down the coast. Suitably rejuvenated, and sensing we had saved the best for last, we set out early one morning to make the three-hour drive to Aphrodisias. We checked out of our hotel in Ismir, and would find a place closer to our goal.

For centuries, the farmers of that area have uncovered pieces of statues and fragments of columns as they plowed their fields. Often they would use them as stone in building their homes. Beautifully carved sarcophagi found their way into barnyards as watering troughs for cattle. It was only in the 1960s that excavations on the site were methodically undertaken. The town of Geyre, which had developed over Aphrodisias, was moved several miles away, and archaeologists began to tackle the enormous task of uncovering what had for so long remained buried. Founded in the 5th century BC by the Greeks, and later expanded by the Romans, it was named for Aphrodite, the goddess of sensual love, fertility, and femininity. A flourishing center for sculpture, at times it supported a population of 60,000. Aphrodisias was finally abandoned in the 7th century AD, and silt from a nearby river covered and protected what remained. As excavations progressed it became apparent that this was truly a center for the arts. A great marble quarry supplied the stone, and signatures on sculpture match those found throughout the Roman world. The work from Aphrodisias is distinguished by its realism and attention to detail. Today, surely to the envy of bigger and more prestigious institutions, their small museum is overflowing with magnificent carvings.

As we approached Geyre, even at a distance we could see the stately columns of the temple of Aphrodite. This time we visited the museum first, and then began to walk the ancient roads. Like Pompeii, much remains to be uncovered, but the site is already so extensive that we spent several hours wandering through the buildings. First to be seen is a stadium in nearly perfect condition, seating 30,000. In similar repair is a beautiful outdoor theater and a small concert hall. We walked to the public baths, the temple, the newer Byzantine city walls, and a ceremonial gate.

There is an unfinished feel to Aphrodisias; the work is still very much in progress, and one often must walk over uneven workmen's rubble, and around temporary plastic fencing. But there is an excitement in the disarray and in feeling almost a part of the archaeological dig. Where and when would the next great sculpture or building be uncovered?

Over dinner that evening we wondered when we could make time to visit a few more ancient Greek and Roman cities. Let's see . . . there is Didyma, Sardis, Troy, Miletus, Priene, Antioch, Side, Aspendos, Perge, Assos . . .

More of the
Greeks and Romans

THE SOUTHERN COAST OF TURKEY, recently dubbed the Turquoise Coast because of its beautiful water, is an area so rich in history that nearly every town showcases interesting reminders of the past. Phoenicians, Egyptians, Greeks, Lycians, Romans, Byzantines and Crusaders all came to these shores and left their mark.

The old town of Kas, toward the western end of the coast, is a particularly pleasant place, situated at the foot of a mountain along the shores of a wide bay. It has enough guest houses and restaurants to make one's stay comfortable, but it is not yet overrun with tourists. Some of its cobblestone streets are narrow and steep, and lined with old Ottoman-style half-timbered houses, but all lead down to a broad, flat harbor promenade. We were here for several days, spending our time hiking to a Greek theater and Lycian tombs in the hills behind the town, and visiting the artisan's shops. And it was here that we hired a boat to take us, and perhaps a dozen other passengers, to the island of Kekova. We had seen our share of Roman ruins but this promised a view with a difference. We would swim and snorkel to see steps, walls, columns and mosaics long submerged as a result of earthquakes.

Lunch and several stops were on the all-day agenda. The weather was clear and warm, the water smooth, and as we left, the Greek island of Kastellorizon was clearly visible in the distance. When we looked back at Kas, the strange rock tombs of the Lycians seemed to hang suspended on the hill above the town.

Our wooden boat had bright blue awnings to shield us from too much sun, and it plodded along for nearly an hour. At our first stop, we were greeted by women in rowboats who passed large baskets filled with hand-embroidered head scarves up to us. Some of the passengers bought the lovely pieces.

The crew handed out snorkels, masks, and fins, pointed us in the direction of the underwater ruins, and into the water we went. We saw nothing at first; then very close to the boat, someone spotted the edge of a ramp, later some steps, and as we swam closer to the shore, we could discern the round bases and pieces of columns, partially submerged doorways, and walls. Along the shore, the structures seemed to emerge and march up the steep hill. The water was calm and warm, and we floated face down for some time, enjoying our "aerial" view of this roofless town. As we paddled along over the buildings, it seemed like every child's daydream of flying.

When we were finally able to tear ourselves away from this secret world, we found that back on the boat, the crew had lit charcoal fires for our lunch. Once we were underway again, we feasted on traditional sis kebab—pieces of lamb and vegetables threaded onto skewers—over rice.

Just as we finished, the boat pulled into a dock at a tiny town named Kale. A dozen or so Lycian rock tombs sat right along the water's edge. Houses, small restaurants, and shops lay along paths that climbed steeply up the hill. There seemed to be no vehicles of any kind, and we thought perhaps that this village was accessible only by water. We could see parts of a crenellated castle wall at the crest, and we guessed that whatever is visible today is only the top half of what was once a larger town. In all probability, the rock tombs at the water line were built high on the hill.

Starting our climb for a closer inspection, we arrived, panting, some time later at the Crusader castle on the summit. From there we had a fantastic view of the mainland, harbor and offshore islands. Nestled inside the old walls was a small Roman theater. In this inaccessible and remote corner of Turkey, on a small mountaintop poking out of the sea, the Lycians, Greeks, Romans, and Crusaders had all left their mark.

We walked down the steep lanes past Ottoman-style houses, through yards hung with laundry, and finally to the small waterfront. It had been an exhilarating day, but the return boat trip seemed long, we were tired, and it was good to get back to Kas.

The next morning we continued our drive east along the coast, and by early afternoon had reached Antalya, a bustling modern city built upon Greek and Roman Attaleia. We entered the city through a great triple arched gate built during the reign of Emperor Hadrian. Just beyond the gate is the old Ottoman quarter, full of recently restored homes and shops. Their intricate balconies of rich dark wood hang over cobblestone streets. We sampled a strangely elastic Turkish ice cream which was made, we were told, with mastic, and bought several blue good luck beads in this charming town within a town.

Later we walked to the Greco-Roman ramparts which run along cliffs overlooking a broad bay. These high fortifications, and the natural harbor they protect, have made Antalya an important city for over two thousand years. Beautiful yachts fill the slips today. We walked through the park along the top for a long distance, watched boys diving from rocks far below, and inspected an ancient stone tower thought to be a Roman lighthouse.

From there the walls curve around the harbor, and we continued until we came at last to a restaurant. Its terrace, which was, in fact, the top of the fortification, held some tables with striped umbrellas linked together by strands of twinkling lights. We seated ourselves at one of these outdoor tables. The effect was magical: a setting sun, a cool breeze, an historic and evocative setting, sailboats resting in a snug harbor below, and wonderful Turkish food. That evening we ate an unusual beef and yogurt soup, plus lamb and peppers over rice. Before leaving, we peeked into the fortress behind us that housed the main dining room of the restaurant. It felt like the castle it was, with high vaulted stone ceilings and Turkish antiques surrounding the diners.

The old market area beckoned the next morning. It was fun to look at the local food and handicraft items. We bought some simit, flaky borek, and fruit for our lunch, eating as we walked along.

Then we were once again off, still traveling east, and planning to arrive by mid-afternoon at another old coastal town called Side. The shore road offered rewarding views of the sea to the right and orange groves to the left.

Side was founded thousands of years ago by the Greeks, built up by the Romans, and recently rediscovered for its fine beaches and profusion of ancient riches. Surrounded by many small inns and sprawling resorts, the mainly Roman buildings are packed onto a promontory near the water. Most spectacular is the amphitheater, which inexplicably faces inland away from the water view, a great semicircle with its high back to the beach. A climb to the top gives one a view of the sea behind, the town below, and the countryside. Clustered in the streets around its base are Roman baths, temples, city walls with gates and towers, fountains, and houses.

We spent several days here, enjoying both the beaches and antiquity. Although the main sites were fascinating, they were far too crowded with tour buses. Luckily, we soon discovered that there were parts of Roman Side literally poking out of the fields, sand dunes, and little country roads all over the area. Even the rim of our hotel pool was lined with column fragments, no doubt uncovered during construction. After viewing the major ruins, we hopped in the car and drove on dirt roads and country lanes to glimpse quieter aspects of Side.

One last pleasant surprise awaited us. Our hotel had a once a week "Turkish Night." Guests there told us to expect a lavish and delicious buffet. Promptly at seven we were seated at an outdoor table with a charming Danish archaeologist and his wife, sipped some raki with them and spoke of his job on a dig to the north in Isparta, which had brought them to Turkey. Then our table was called and we walked into the dining room. Many tables were placed end to end in a giant horseshoe and covered with perhaps seventy or eighty platters and hot trays of beautifully arranged and presented foods. Wherever there was a bit of space, fresh flowers and leaves from the hotel gardens were placed directly on the linen table cloths. Great cornucopia of fruits and vegetables occupied strategic locations. The total effect was altogether striking.

We began with a plate of assorted meze, returned to sample one of the soups, and then in proper Turkish fashion, came back again and again, each time with a fresh plate, for small skewers of grilled meat and fish, cold vegetable dishes, pilavs, and finally desserts. The sweets especially were lovely, arranged on doilies, each one a sparkling jewel of honey, nuts, and pastry. In addition there were puddings, compotes, and candies.

We chatted with the couple from Denmark about the work of archaeologists in uncovering the past and about our interest in these areas. The soft summer evening filled with good conversation and good food was the perfect conclusion to several days spent viewing Side's past. The next day we would begin a drive north into the heart-land of Turkey. We had heard of a great salt lake, underground dwellings, and churches carved into hillsides. We wanted to see these wonders for ourselves.

Amazing Cappadocia

MILLIONS OF YEARS AGO, at the very center of Turkey, in an area called Cappadocia, violent volcanic eruptions poured rivers of lava onto hundreds of square miles. Over time, water and wind eroded the high flat land of soft volcanic mud and ash into a fantastic moonscape of deep ravines and tall cones. Rock colors look faded in the strong sun, and range from stark white, through the softest pastels of yellow, pink, purple and tan.

Four thousand years ago the Hittites were among the earliest to discover that the stone had properties as magical as its look. It was soft enough to be carved with primitive tools and hardened on contact with air. Snug dwellings could be cut with ease. Over the millennia all manner of churches, homes, and entire towns have been fashioned from the cooperative material. As we were to discover, it is a landscape unlike any other. The bleached and pale valley stretches as far as the eye can see. In many areas the higher outcroppings are so riddled with doorways, arches, and windows that they look like giant sponges. In other places, dozens of inverted cones, known as "fairy chimneys," each with a dark, delicately balanced capstone, seem to march along in unison.

Cappadocia has many roads, small villages, and much to see, so we planned to stay for some days. Urgup is a town centrally located on a main crossroad in the area, and most of its buildings are at least partially hewn from the living rock. We decided to stay at a hotel cut into the mountainside. The rooms and dining room were definitely cavelike, and niches took the place of shelves and some furniture. Predictably, it was pleasantly cool inside, and it became our headquarters for a few days.

Christianity came early to these valleys and ravines, and literally hundreds of small churches, chapels, and monastic cells were created in the stone. The dozen or so we visited are accessible by clambering up gravel paths and climbing steps cut into the rock. Once inside, we were able to view the frescoes painted on vaulted ceilings many centuries ago. Most paintings have the saints' faces scratched out, the work of hundreds of devout Moslems over the ages, who wished to obliterate the hated images. But Christian communities persisted here, deep in Cappadocia, until the 20th century.

Each town in the area is unique. All are small, most are farming communities (the white sand here is apparently quite fertile), and all are worth a visit. We took winding roads up to abandoned towns carved high into the hills, drove into towns still full of Greek style houses from the 19th century, and found one village of pottery studios and shops. We were unable to resist buying several lovely small vases, but when we went inside to pay, the proprietor wanted locks of our hair, too! Hanging from the ceiling and walls were thousands of strands of hair attached to signed cards from all over the world. We had never seen anything quite like it, and got in on the fun with our own donations.

But the most truly astonishing towns of Cappadocia are underground. By 700 AD the first Arab armies had begun their mission of conversion, and early Christians, already well established, began to tunnel and dig straight down into the soft stone to hide. In time an extensive network of entire cities extended down as many as eight stories below ground, and were home to 60,000 people. We visited one of the two cities that have been excavated. Climbing down into the labyrinth of gray rock pathways is both frightening and fascinating. Levels and directions are indistinct, and one must crouch in passageways. Some spaces are clearly communal, large eating halls for example, and some are small private family rooms. Deep wells and air shafts fall away into blackness. It would be easy to become lost in this gigantic rock sponge, and we found it hard to believe that thousands lived here for years at a time, hidden away from their enemies. It was depressingly cold and dark, and definitely not a place for claustrophobics. For 20th century visitors there are arrows painted on the walls, and a few electric lights to guide the way; but we were relieved to be out in the sunshine once again.

Ancient caravan roads crisscross Cappadocia, and during the Seljuk and Ottoman periods numerous hans or inns, also called caravanserais, were built along these routes to offer shelter to man, beast, and goods. They were often built by one or another sultan to encourage trade and as prestigious public works. Each has a similar plan. They are massive and impregnable compounds, round or square; with rooms, stables and warehouses around the inside periphery, and an enormous inner open air courtyard sheltering an obligatory mosque. The entrances are typically embellished with arches, tiles, and elaborate stonework. As we were leaving the Cappadocian region we routed ourselves so as to visit three of these caravan shelters. They're visible from some miles away, in every case standing majestically alone on the dusty and barren land. We could imagine the long ago parades of camels, loaded with trade items from the East, led by their handlers, inching their way toward the sheltering han.

We wanted to see one more natural wonder before leaving the area—the great salt lake of Tuz Golu. The second largest lake in Turkey, it only has a thin slick of water in winter. In summer it is a blindingly white and absolutely flat pan of salt, forty miles long, which lies beside the main road to Ankara. At first, at the south edges of the lake there are marshes and some standing water, but as we drove along, the water gradually disappeared, and finally, only salt could be seen. We stopped the car where the road ran closest to the "lake," and began to gingerly walk out onto the salt. Its appearance was like snow, but it was hard and firm. People, looking like dots, walked at least a mile out. We poked a finger into the surface, and a tiny puddle filled the depression. The water of winter had evaporated to just below the surface. We walked and played on the salt for some time, exhilarated by the sight and the strong wind that blew from the distant mountains. Then we returned to the car and continued our drive to Ankara.

Exploring the North Coast

THE BLACK SEA STRETCHES along nearly all of Turkey's northern edge, and except for the region around Istanbul, it is little developed or explored. At its far eastern end lies the port of Trabzon. We flew there from Istanbul one autumn day. Our plan was to rent a car and drive west, stopping at the many historic little towns and sights along the way.

Trabzon was founded nearly 3,000 years ago. Its ancient citadel or kale sits on a promontory of rock facing a large curving bay. On that first day, we checked into a hotel on the main square in town. Then we visited the citadel, crossing a ravine by bridge and walking up the steep roads into its center. Large portions of the old walls remain, and the streets inside this well fortified site are predictably narrow. Small half-timbered shops and homes line the cobblestone lanes.

From there we walked to the lower town, nearly as old as the citadel. This is where farmers bring their produce, to a central market already in full swing when we arrived. The country women of northeastern Turkey wear colorful outfits that include a sort of wraparound head scarf. One giggling and shy woman seated behind stacks of fresh produce let us snap her portrait.

The variety of food on display was staggering. Fresh seafood of all kinds lay in glistening profusion on traditional round red wooden trays. There were pastries, nuts, beans, meat, fruit, vegetables, olives, herbs, and spices for sale that day. The climate in the eastern Black Sea region is one of sunny summers, moderate winters, and abundant rainfall. It is a center for fishing, and the specialized growing of tea, tobacco, cherries, and hazelnuts, plus all manner of everyday fruits and vegetables, including cabbages fully fifteen inches in diameter. All of the produce was arranged with pride; even the roasted chestnuts were stacked in precise pyramids.

At the edge of the market area a small restaurant served grilled kofte and shepherd's salad for lunch. After eating we visited Ayasofia, a Byzantine church situated on a green hill overlooking the sea, about two miles outside of town. The 13th century frescos there are well preserved and quite fine. As the sun began to set we drove to Ataturk's summer cottage, a Victorian villa overlooking the Black Sea. Now a museum, the house was a present from the people of Trabzon to the father of modern Turkey.

That evening, a slow chugging taxi took us up a steep hill to a recommended restaurant overlooking Trabzon. Set in a pine woods high above the city, a half dozen small private pavilions are arranged at the ends of paths leading from the main dining room. Each affords a view of the Black Sea where it meets the land, to form a perfect crescent-shaped necklace of lights far below.

We began dinner with the traditional assorted meze. Our waiter carried an enormous tray of perhaps twenty small plates to our pavilion. We chose three; cacik, fried peppers and eggplant, and vegetable fritters. For our main course we shared some tomato pilav and grilled lamb kebabs. The breezes were warm, even well into October, and the noises of the town drifted faintly up to us.

Before leaving the next morning we enjoyed a regional breakfast of cherry juice, tea, several local cheeses, fresh yogurt, and bread. Then one hour of driving on a winding and beautiful road brought us to the ruins of the 14th century Sumela monastery. Perched on a steep mountain cliff face in a cool pine forest, it is thirty miles south of Trabzon. When one can drive no farther, cars are left below. It takes another hour of climbing up the steep and narrow path to reach the top. We paused many times along the way to catch our breath and enjoy the view. A set of steps clings to the outside of the monastery wall as a daunting last barrier before gaining entrance. Inside is what appears to be a tiny village made up of postage stamp-sized court-yards and individual monk's cells. A chapel wedged under a rocky outcropping is covered on the outside with beautiful frescos. The view of the forests and distant mountains shrouded in clouds was spectacular. Save for a single caretaker, we were alone in this pious and isolated retreat from long ago.

After leaving the Sumela monastery we continued south and crossed the ridge of mountains in northern Turkey which separate the Black Sea from the central plains. The change is dramatic. To the north are lush orchards, tea plantations, farms, and deep forests. To the south, over the pass, it is dry and dusty, the mountains having stopped the rain clouds generated by the sea. Flocks of sheep take the place of green terraced farms.

We drove through the sere landscape for a long time. Distances are deceiving in the absence of trees and buildings. Only the hundreds of sheep that appeared as tiny dots helped us gauge the miles that stretched before us. The colors are all subtle pinks, browns, white and tans, with vegetation so sparse and low that the smooth, sensually rolling land appears to be covered in velvet.

We stopped in a town called Gumushane, to eat a lunch of lamb kebabs over white beans and rice. Once an important trading center along the route between Trabzon and Iran, today its faded charm can be seen in the old style architecture of its houses and mosques. We attracted considerable attention as we walked the streets of this seldom visited outpost. In the schoolyard a teacher gathered her entire class of uniformed young girls and motioned for us to snap their portrait.

That afternoon we drove on to Bayburt, which also lay along the ancient Silk Road, to see the castle there. As we entered the town we could see a Byzantine fortress stretching for some distance along the top of a hill at the far end of the main street. Stopping to ask a grocer directions, we were surprised when he immediately left his shop, motioned for us to follow and hopped into his friend's car. We stayed close behind as they led the way up a long, rough, dusty road to the castle. We passed small houses, where women dressed in the local costume of brown and blue shawls sat in doorways keeping an eye on their playing children. At one point our car lost traction in the deep sand. At last we were inside the walls. A field trip of schoolgirls were the only other visitors, but they laughed and hid their faces behind long shawls when we waved. We stayed for some time and watched the sun set behind the mountains.

Finally our guides led us back to town and into the grocery store for tea. We exchanged addresses, took photos, promised to write, and then were given a bag of pomegranates, apples, and grapes to take with us.

It was almost dark and too late to drive back across the mountains to the coast, so we took a room. As we strolled around the pleasant streets that evening, literally dozens of young people approached us and introduced themselves, saying that they just wanted to speak a few words of English. The people of Bayburt were proving to be unusually curious, hospitable and generous!

Later, we were the only outsiders at a charming restaurant where we feasted on regional specialties. Dessert was cooked fruit compote with roasted chopped hazelnuts and small glasses of fresh cherry juice.

The next morning we returned to the Black Sea coast after our one day excursion inland. Continuing west, we drove along the water for some miles, past old stone farm houses. Farmyards and front porches groaned under the weight of mountains of harvested melons and squash, thousands of ears of bright yellow corn strung up to dry, and tobacco leaves draped onto long poles. Cut corn stalks were piled in the crooks of trees which seemed unaffected by their "tan balloons" of drying vegetation. Women brightly dressed in long skirts and lace-bordered head scarves led fat brown cows in ones and twos to pasture.

That night we stopped in Samsun and the next day continued west toward Sinop. We enjoyed extraordinary vistas of the coast, the aqua and blue sea to one side, green hills to the other. The farms here were much bigger than those we had seen the day before, resembling the large corn, wheat, and vegetable fields of Ohio and New York. Tall white minarets dotted the landscape on this sunny autumn day. Our stop at Sinop included visits to their citadel, whose ancient walls overlook a wonderful natural harbor, to the old fisherman's quarter along the shore, and to the archaeological museum with its Greek temple.

That evening we stayed in the small beach town of Cide and got an early start the following morning in order to drive to the picturesque port of Amasra for breakfast. Strangely situated on a narrow peninsula and guarded by ancient Byzantine fortifications at its headland, Amasra actually has two harbors, facing east and west. It was a peaceful Sunday morning, blue, clear and cool. Fishermen on the sandy beach repaired nets and small, neatly painted dories. Breakfast that day was a pure Turkish delight, and simple as it was, sticks in our minds as one of the most memorable. Hot strong Turkish coffee, and fragrant Black Sea tea arrived first. Sweet slabs of butter, hazelnut jelly, rose petal jelly, salty olives, and fresh bland cheese were arranged on large plates. The bakery next door supplied still warm bread, and we probably ate a loaf apiece before staggering out onto the street again.

From Amasra we planned to visit two towns noted for their Ottoman architecture. Here the coast road climbs high above the shore. Hairpin turns, narrow lanes, and our constant stops for photos made the journey slow. Everywhere in the lush green mountain landscape are old Ottoman bridges and castles, ravines crossed by thin rickety footbridges, and tiny terraced farms clinging to high alpine meadows. It is easy to understand the purity and isolation of the area. Even today there is only this one difficult road.

At last we arrived at the first destination, Bartin, a pretty village of half-timbered houses. We walked its streets, peered into shops, took photos, and ate lentil soup and pide for lunch.

Further on, Safranbolu, the second town of old houses, had begun a restoration project. Here the half-timbered dwellings sported a fresh coat of white stucco. They lined cobblestone streets worn shiny with age. The two-story white and brown houses contrast with the shops on other streets. The all wood commercial buildings are unpainted and weathered to dark brown. Wide, low eaves overhang the narrow lanes there, and men sit outside playing board games in this warren of old, tiny shops. Nearby, bakers use long paddles to pull hundreds of fresh loaves out of ovens. Along one street, restoration had begun on a han (inn) from Safranbolu's old trading route days. It was peaceful and pretty here in a town trying to preserve and honor its past, while remaining alive today.

Our next stop would be Istanbul. It had been a rewarding five-day trip into an area of great beauty and fascination. In the 3,000 years since the first Greek settlements little has changed. As in the rest of Turkey, empires here come and go, but the mountains have set this Black Sea area apart and helped make its people self-sufficient but friendly. As a man who brought us tea one day in a small town said, "We just like to talk to visitors."

Repaying a Favor

ONE MORNING WHILE DRIVING in southern Turkey, we passed a large truck loaded with oranges pulled off to the side of the road. Three men clustered around the open hood, peering expectantly at the engine. On a whim we stopped. Unfortunately, stopping to help a stranger can be a dangerous pastime at home, but after some weeks of travel in Turkey we were so struck by the honesty and friendliness of the people, that we decided to take a chance. We were not wrong.

We speak not one word of Turkish, and the three stranded truckers knew no English, so all the communications for the next several hours that we were destined to remain together took place with a strange mixture of signs, drawn symbols, map reading, gestures, and lots of smiles, patience, and good will.

They "explained" to us that their truck, carrying a load of oranges from the groves along the Mediterranean coast, had broken down on its way to market. Would it be possible to give two of them a lift back to their hometown? The third man would stay behind to guard the truck and its cargo. They found their village for us on our map. It was only a short side road out of our way, and we agreed to take them there. The two climbed into the back seat, and in the hour it took to reach their hometown, we learned that they were both married and each had children; and we told them where we were from and about our family. Photos were shown around, and we accepted an invitation to have tea with them when we arrived.

Once we were close, it took several miles of twisting and turning on dirt roads until we were actually in the village. It was quite poor and primitive. Main street (the only street) was unpaved, and lined with the simplest unpainted wooden structures. Our lone vehicle was the subject of much curiosity from a dozen children. They gathered around our car in a flash when they saw the two familiar men climb out of the back seat. The little boys—there were no females of any age in sight—found our sunglasses most amusing; laughing and pointing, they motioned to try them on.

We were invited to cross the street to the local outdoor tea shop, and were immediately seated at a simple table. Steaming glasses of tea arrived, a small crowd of men gathered, and we were bombarded with gestured questions. Were we married? To each other? Did we have children? Where were they? Where did we live? Why were we in Turkey?

Time passed quickly, and it was clear that they felt that a glass of tea was insufficient payment for the favor we had done. Another young man materialized and motioned for us to take him in our car to see some special sight. At the end of town he took us down a country lane and up to a hill. On it were five beautifully preserved Lycian rock tombs. The Lycians lived in the area of southern Turkey about 3,000 years ago, and there are many examples of their funerary architecture in the area. The tombs look somewhat like the fronts of miniature Greek temples, recessed into the rock surface from which they are cut.

We climbed up the hill followed by our new friend, who was obviously proud to show us his village's piece of ancient history. These were the first tombs of the many that we had visited that we could see at such close hand, and even walk into, so we especially appreciated his effort to bring us here.

Later, when we were about to leave, our guide became very insistent that we go one more place with him. Even though we needed to be on our way, our curiosity overcame our sense of time, and we allowed him to lead us, by car, another half mile or so along the same dirt road to a wooded area. A small circular structure, with a shallow dome for a roof, sat beside a stream there. Five window openings were spaced around the outer wall. They were secured with large mesh grating, and tied to these grates were hundreds of bits of cloth and string. We had passed similar structures from time to time along roads in Turkey, and were always puzzled by them. We had guessed that they were granaries, but were soon to find out that they were shrines and mausoleums for Islamic holy men, the saints and teachers of their religion.

Our new friend invited us through the open door. The only object in the room was a large stone coffin with a turban on top. Additional pieces of torn cloth were everywhere. Through pantomime we thought we understood that the cloth tatters were left by each visitor as a token of sadness. We later learned this to be somewhat correct, that the tearing and tying of bits of one's clothing are a reminder to the saint of a favor asked.

Then our friend guided us over to the stream, where a small watermelon was cooling. Motioning us to sit on some rocks, and to keep clear of the nibblings of several goats tied nearby, he treated us to an expert demonstration of melon sectioning. Using a pocketknife, he removed a circular cap from one end and set it aside. Next, he made six vertical cuts in the rind. Inverting the melon cut side down on the melon cap, he struck a sharp blow to the top, and it split into a half dozen neat wedges. We are quite sure this act is not to be duplicated on the dining room table at home, but it seemed the perfect method here. We were handed big slices, dripping with juice. There we sat on rocks by a stream, "speaking" with a stranger turned friend, and fending off pushy goats. No melon ever tasted better.

It had turned out to be such an enriching day. We helped some folks, and they had taken considerable trouble to reciprocate by sharing some tea, their humble town with its interesting Lycian past and Islamic present, and their warm smiles and curiosity. Instead of just "viewing" a country, we felt that we had in a small way made some people-to-people connections, and we were charmed by their graciousness.

A Ferry Up the Bosporus

ONE OF THE LEAST EXPENSIVE and most rewarding bits of sightseeing one can do in and around Istanbul is to take an all-day
ride on one of the public ferries which serve the three sections of the
city. The "old" and "new" cities on the continent of Europe, and the
eastern suburbs in Asia, are divided by the Bosporus Strait, the Golden
Horn, and, to the south, the Sea of Marmara. Most ferries leave from
docks along the Golden Horn on the old city side, and make short
trips back and forth between there and the Asian suburbs, but others go all the way up the Bosporus nearly to the Black Sea, stopping
alternately at towns along both sides of the waterway before returning. This longer trip was the one we planned to take.

We bought a ticket the night before after checking schedules and
destinations, and that morning dawned cool and sunny. There are far
too many attractions along the way to see in one day, so we picked
just two places to disembark, promising ourselves to try to see at least
a few of the rest by land another time.

Leaving the city proper by boat is exciting in itself, allowing
another chance to gaze upon that famous skyline before leaving it
behind. Across the Golden Horn, the new city, situated along the
slope of a gentle hill, also has its attractions. The most noticeable is
the Galata Tower, built in 1348, and the enormous ships docked at
its waterfront.

We quickly left old and new Istanbul behind, and began traveling
up the Bosporus. Both shores of this winding strait are a feast for the

eyes, offering up sights in a delightful mix of past and present, grand splendor and simple beauty. For the entire distance we could view shore front wooden villas, great marble palaces, stone fortresses, and small villages.

The first unforgettable sight is Dolmabahçe Palace, stretching for 2,000 feet along the European shore. It was built in the 19th century in a last gasp of Ottoman opulence. We had visited its vast and showy halls and gardens earlier, but the view from the water stunned us with its size.

Stretching for another mile or two along the same shore is another palace, vast public gardens, and a grand hotel. If one is traveling this way on a Sunday, artists gather at a street fair at the next stop (Ortakoy) to show their work each week. Immensely overshadowing Ortakoy is the Bosporus Bridge. One of the world's largest suspension bridges, it links Europe and Asia. We passed slowly, far beneath it.

Another beautiful showplace, Beylerbeyi Palace, lies just past the bridge on the Asian side, and behind it rises Camlica Hill, the highest point in the city. We had heard that the view from the delightful park on the top is the best in Istanbul, and we hoped to make a separate trip there.

We were passing wooden Ottoman villas along the European shore now. Called "yali," each one is unique, yet similar, in their intricate and ornate woodwork. They are built with balconies hanging over the water's edge, and most have boat docks or boat houses.

Past the villas, facing each other across the waterway like sentries guarding the city, stand the fortresses of Rumeli Hisari and Anadolu Hisari. These formidable fortifications were built in a matter of months in 1451, and were instrumental in bringing about the final defeat of the Byzantine Empire in 1453. Rumeli can be visited for a small fee and this, too, we would try to fit into our plans for another day. Our ferry passed a second bridge, a park and a palace, and then we were pulling into our first stop. On the Asian shore is the one time fishing village of Kanlica, now a wealthy suburb of elegant villas. Ever on the quest for delicious food, we learned that this small town was renowned for its yogurt. This then would be our lunch stop. The waterfront still retains much of the flavor of its older, less posh days, and cafés and restaurants line the shore. We disembarked, and knew we could catch the next boat north in about an hour. We chose a small restaurant right on the narrow promenade next to the water.

In Turkey, in some types of eateries, items are chosen by sight rather than by menu, with the food displayed in the great flat pans in which it is cooked. Here the famous yogurt was also displayed in the large trays in which it had fermented. Indicating that we hoped they would serve us manageably small portions, we picked several meze, and a dish of spicy yogurt with garlic. Nibbling on small bits of fried liver and onions, grilled mussels on skewers, and fried eggplant strips, all dipped in the garlicky yogurt mix, was heavenly. The yogurt was unusually thick, tangy, and rich. We returned to the serving counter and chose some sliced roast lamb over rice, this time accompanied by a kind of cucumber and yogurt sauce, perfect with the salty meat. For dessert we had fresh cantaloupe served with firm yogurt (drained of its whey) drizzled with honey.

Well satisfied with our "yogurt with everything" lunch, we had to hurry to get on the next boat. Our second and final goal for the day was the village of Sariyer, the last stop for ferries before the Black Sea. We wanted to visit a special museum there and see life in a relatively quiet Bosporus town.

For a while we continued to pass yacht basins, villas, taverns, and fish restaurants along the shore, but then, more rural pursuits came into view—boys swimming from unused docks, and lone men fishing from small boats. At last we were at Sariyer. Street vendors were ready for the boats, selling simit, roasted corn, cotton candy, roasted nuts of all kinds, and grilled mussels—four to a wooden skewer.

The museum of Sadberk Hanim is a short distance along the shore south of the dock. It is housed in a cheery, clean, yellow and white house, and had a marvelous and intimate collection of artifacts from Neolithic Anatolia through the Roman period. Everything is beautifully displayed and labeled, and we thought the pieces were some of the best we had ever seen. Of special note were pieces of exquisite Roman jewelry.

It was late when we were finished viewing the exhibits, and we strolled along the waterfront, stopping to look into shops, and sat on a bench to watch the people.

When we calculated we had only one hour left until the last ferry back, we found a restaurant for dinner. One of the most famous of all Turkish meat dishes is Circassian Chicken. It is chicken smothered in a ground walnut sauce and usually served with one or another pilav. We had never tried it and so we were happy to find it on the menu. The waiter brought a small dish of olives, but having overdone it a bit on lunch, we ordered no other meze. Our chicken dish was a surprise, not because it was delicious, but because we did not realize that it is always served cold. Cooked, boned, chicken pieces are covered in a garlicky purée of walnuts, stock, and bread. We ordered a simple tomato and cucumber salad to accompany the main dish, sipped some beer, and watched the boat traffic on the Bosporus.

Soon our hour was over, and the boat appeared to take us to the city. On the return trip we sat in the back, and let the sights pass in reverse. An enormous Turkish flag, red field with white crescent and star, snapped in the breeze off the stern.

Country Markets

URKISH PEOPLE LOVE to buy and sell. In this country, more than in any other we have ever visited, the spirit of entrepreneurship is a mark of their culture, and, we're sure they believe, of civilization itself. It is, of course, like everywhere else, how goods are distributed and how some people make their living. But in modern Anatolia, sitting as it does astride the ancient caravan routes of trade, it has been raised to an art form. Every street corner hosts an open air business, and every niche holds a small shop. The creativity of street vendor food is a daily treat. Ingenious devices strapped to backs and shoulders allow drinks and trinkets to be carried to the customer. There is even a market for once-read newspapers to circulate again before the news is too old.

This spirited buying and selling makes the once or twice weekly markets in small towns all over Turkey a particular delight. They are virtually impossible to plan ahead for, and so we are always happy to chance upon one. We have been to so many that they tend to blur together for us, so our clearest reminder is often just a photo, or something we purchased. Best are the ones discovered when we are hungry because there is always a bag of olives, roasted almonds or dried apricots to be bought, or hot simit or borek to eat as we walk along.

We remember in particular one rather large gathering. We guessed it to be regional because the town was small, and on the roads leading to it were parked small trucks, wagons, and carts. We found a place to park, and waded into the crowds. The streets were informally divided by type of goods, and we started in the food market. This street was lined with houses; small, stucco, and earth colored, with brightly painted windows and doors. There were no yards or sidewalks; their walls came to the edge of the narrow street. Seated on blankets on the ground and leaning against the walls of the houses, were women, heads covered with black or brown scarves, tranquilly sorting and displaying their prized produce. Each had only two or three types to sell, perfect tomatoes, bright green beans, a pyramid of onions, polished eggplants or baskets of cherries. Further along the same street, men seemed to be the ones to handle the vending of small packages of spices, or dried beans and nuts heaped in large burlap sacks. Near one corner, a man stood beside a beautifully painted and decorated flatbed wagon full of a load of pears on a bed of straw. Housewives walked in and out of their doors to haggle and buy, and children hung from windows to watch the action. Young boys delivered tea, never spilling a drop as they darted through the crowd, swinging six full glasses from a small hanging tray.

One or two streets further, in a more open area, were wagons full of household goods. The patient draft horses that pulled them into place were tethered in a nearby field. Many things here were quite utilitarian—pots and pans, plastic containers, shoes and clothing; but also for sale were many hand-crafted articles, which we found fascinating. Piled on carts were carved bowls, wooden ladles and sets of matching soup spoons. In Turkey, soup is considered best when eaten with a wooden spoon, so we bought a large wooden serving spoon and a set of the soup spoons. A little further along, a man had a display of wood and string strainers in several sizes. We bought one, and it hangs to this day on our kitchen wall, but we have never discovered its use. It has a five inch deep bent wooden rim like a Chinese steamer, and is strung like a tennis racket with gut strings. In the center is one blue good luck bead. The strings are too spaced to sift flour, the sides are too high to winnow wheat, and bread dough would ooze through before it raised. Perhaps it is used for drying or smoking; we're sure someday, someone will give us the answer.

Nearby, several rope vendors displayed their beautifully handmade products along the pavement. They were creating rope of various sizes by twisting hemp fibers together. We watched, in fascination, as such a basic product was being lovingly created by three old men. We walked past men and boys assembling simple wooden furniture, mostly stools, small tables, benches, and chairs. They whittled ends of rungs to fit into legs, and cut and planed pieces to fit.

Soon we entered a part of the market that on non-market days appeared to be the commercial, rather than the residential, end of town. Small shops lined the cobblestone road, and proprietors had set out tables in front, with their wares. Others had wheeled in carts full of goods just for market day. Everything for sale here was old. Used tools and utensils, carpets, tiles, coins, pots and pans were tumbled together in the confusion of a gigantic tag sale. This, for us, was the most interesting part of the market. We wandered and looked, and ended up buying too many wonderful old Turkish artifacts. The first purchase was an antique aqua and white tile covered with Arabic calligraphy. We also bought Ottoman coins and a beautiful coffee pot. The pot is fifteen inches high; tall, curvy and graceful, with a hinged lid and a tiny spout. Stamped on the handle is a date. The man who sold it to us made the conversion from the Islamic year to the Christian calendar. Our pot is about seventy years old. The original copper has worn through its tinning in spots, and it has a lovely patina of age. Our last purchase that day was a bowl, about ten inches across, also tinned over the original copper. Its flat bottom, two inches deep, is covered with geometric designs, and around the rim is a row of flower-like symbols. It was beautifully crafted long ago, with a slim foot soldered to the bottom.

Turkey has many attractions for the traveler, and along with its other attributes, it is most certainly an absolute shopper's paradise. Unique and striking items are everywhere, and in more provincial areas, the prices are reasonable. Bargaining is always appropriate, even expected. Indeed, the process itself seems to further ignite the entrepreneurial spirit of the merchants, and they are experts at it. For us, it adds to the fun and adventure, and in other markets, at other times and places, we have had a chance to hone our skills.

One purchase, that actually stretched over two days, involved a woven baby cradle. We had seen ones like it from time to time in handicraft museums, and in displays of nomadic artifacts, and so when we spotted one in a regional market, we were ready to buy. The good bargainer always makes a casual price inquiry and then feigns disinterest. The price was really too high, and now our part of the process demanded that we point out every fault of the piece, look intently at other pieces, and leave to go to other shops. But we returned once or twice, and so by the next day when the proprietor looked up to see our faces again, he immediately sent a boy out for tea. We must be serious about something in his shop. Had he guessed it was the cradle piece? In proper Turkish fashion, conversation did not turn to business until we had spent several minutes exchanging pleasantries over the hot sweet tea. Then we offered to pay half of what was originally asked for the cradle. Looking insulted, he suggested a price that was only a bit lower than the original, we thanked him for the tea, and started to leave. Of course he wouldn't let us go, and a couple of price exchanges later we settled on an amount a few dollars more than our first offer. We were sure that was the price he intended to sell it for all along! Handshakes, smiles, and then we emerged from the shop happily clutching the cradle. Today it hangs in our entranceway, a beautiful piece of rich reds and blues, with exuberant tassels all around.

Since then we have bought handmade copper sheep bells, ceramic candle holders, a set of skewers for sis kebab, purses made from antique kilims, and one day, in Konya, we bought a full-sized living room carpet. But that is another story.

A Modern Capital

ANKARA IS THE VERY MODERN CAPITAL OF TURKEY, established by the country's new leader after the first world war. Kemal Ataturk, the first president of the newly formed republic, chose Ankara over Istanbul because of the military safety of its isolation, and to make a fresh start disassociated with all previous empires. At that time it was a sleepy town involved primarily in the trade of its beautiful wool. The yarn made of unusually long fibers from specially bred goats in that region was known throughout the world. The name Angora (Ankara) is, in fact, the original European name for the wool and the town.

It has grown phenomenally since then, and today is a true government town, with broad tree-lined avenues, skyscrapers, and first class hotels and restaurants. Most of the places we have visited in Turkey are historical or geographical landmarks, unusual ruins or spectacular rock formations. Ankara has little to recommend it in these areas, but lest we forget that Turkey is not entirely rural, we decided to spend several days there. There were two principal attractions and several lesser sights on our list to see.

Driving into the city one comes first to the old city area, still remaining from its pre-capital days. With the exception of a drive to Ataturk's memorial, and a lovely meal in a dining room high atop a hotel in the new section of the city, in the several days we were in Ankara we stayed right within this old section, and walked from place to place. We also discovered that the older hotels there, if not as fancy as the newer ones in the government section of the town, are every bit as pleasant. We settled on one several blocks from the rather noisy main square.

The Museum of Anatolian Civilizations is on everyone's list of a place not to be missed; and its praise is well deserved. We walked through the main square and up a hill past the citadel to the museum. It occupies a building that used to be a han (inn) or caravanserai, and contains the best and most complete exhibit of the arts and artifacts of the Hittites anywhere in the world. It also has collections of pre-historic, Assyrian, Greek and Roman work, all of it tastefully and thoughtfully displayed, and labeled in Turkish and English.

The Hittites founded one of the great civilizations of the Bronze Age in central Anatolia between the 15th and 12th centuries BC. They created great stone fortresses, forceful bas reliefs to enhance them, and many pieces of smaller sculpture of unusual grace and beauty. They could smelt iron, and their formidable fighters threatened the Egyptians. The ruin of their main city at Bogazkale is an easy drive from Ankara, but most of the best that has been found there is in the museum. We spent several hours touring the exhibits, which showed through photographs, how and where a particular find was located, and the process of digging it out. When we saw the actual piece in the museum, the photos gave it much more meaning. We were stunned by room after room of the works of the early Anatolian civilizations, and found ourselves wishing that this was the very first place that we had visited on an earlier trip. Then we could have toured Greek and Roman ruins, finally seeing the Byzantine and Ottoman architecture and arts in Istanbul. We had taken a backwards walk through history and were now busily resorting the pieces.

It was late afternoon when we were finished at the museum, and we would see the citadel, Roman Ankara, and Ataturk's tomb the next day. We had heard of several restaurants at the top of skyscrapers in the new city that offered panoramic views along with good food. After resting and showering at the hotel, we were given the name of one of these restaurants with the "best food in town."

The directions led us to a glittering new hotel. Its lobby is on several levels and the restaurant is on the top floor. We ascended in a high speed elevator and emerged in a lovely dining room. Of course we requested a window seat, and there below was all of Ankara, and the hills beyond. Lights began to twinkle on shortly after we arrived, and as the evening wore on the sky turned to inky star-studded blackness, and the city put on a new face.

Our waiter brought menus, and we ordered stuffed mussels, and fried vegetable pieces with a garlicky dip. Next came a delicious lentil soup for two. We chose one main dish of lamb stew, and the other of spicy grilled ground lamb on a skewer. We shared a large bowl of village or shepherd's salad, and some white wine. For dessert we sampled small sweet cakes in syrup, and an unusual pudding that our waiter assured us contained chicken. The evening was lovely, and we lingered over two tiny cups of Turkish style coffee, gazing down at the city below.

Back down in the lobby, we watched, amused, as a family of five with a traditionally dressed grandmother approached an escalator. The old woman was wearing country clothes—baggy pantaloons and a brightly patterned head scarf. Perhaps she had never seen an escalator before; this was certainly her first ride on one. It took a lot of hand holding, demonstrations and encouragement, but at last she and the others, were on, amid lots of smiles. It reminded us that Ankara was, not very long ago, just a small country town. The next day we drove to the beautiful memorial dedicated to the hero and founder of modern Turkey, Kemal Ataturk. It is situated on a hill overlooking the middle of Ankara. One must walk through a lovely park, past honor guards and sculpture, to the impressive tomb building itself. Inside, under a gold roof, soaring windows overlook the city. In the center rests an immense marble sarcophagus. It is a fitting monument from the Turkish people to the father of their country. We stayed for a while, admiring the splendor and the view, and then walked to some small museum exhibits of Ataturk memorabilia; his cars, personal belongings and photographs. Yesterday we had seen prehistoric and

Hittite Turkey, and now we were viewing the most recent history of this fascinating country. Slowly all the pieces were falling into place.

In the afternoon we left the car at the hotel, and walked the several blocks to the old city area. The center of commercial activity there is called Ulus Square, a bustling, noisy and fascinating monument to the Turkish affinity for buying and selling—everything! Most business seems not to be housed indoors; that would seem too isolating to Turkish sensibilities. Rather, all manner of enterprise takes place from carts, tables, and mats on the street. Food in many varieties, shoe repairs, trinkets, souvenirs, electronics, and clothing can be purchased without entering the big department stores that line the square.

We ate a delicious lunch of the ubiquitous doner kebab. Impossible to duplicate at home, every town has a small shop where one can buy the succulent lamb roasted on a vertical spit, and served with a spicy sauce on fresh rounds of pide bread. After our stand-up meal we slowly wandered up the same road we had taken the day before, and that we knew ran past the citadel.

These old walls were begun by the Romans, added to by Byzantines, and maintained through the early Ottoman period. They lie in two semicircles with a warren of old shops and houses between the two great arcs. To step through the gate is to step back in time. Stones and bits of columns from the oldest Roman ruins have been reused in the buildings on the winding little streets. A line of defensive towers marks the inner fortress. The houses, shops, and markets continue within its walls, spilling out into the large open cobblestoned area at the crest of the hill. We walked back through the streets, and came, at last, to a lane of craftsmen's shops specializing in copper and tin. Browsing through the old and new ware, we bought a small pewter dish, then wandered out of the citadel area and back to Ulus Square.

From there we headed around to the north on the main road for several streets until we arrived in the old Roman district. Not very much remains, nothing of the magnitude of the much more well-known ruins at Ephesus and Pergamum. There is a Roman bath house, a bit further on is the so-called Column of Julian, and the remains of a temple. We looked at it all, still impressed by the far reaching Roman empire. Our guidebook told us that this was an outpost in central Anatolia 2,000 years ago, of perhaps 150,000 citizens, not equaled in size again until the 20th century.

Ankara, so often bypassed in the tour bus itineraries of Turkey, was well worth the several days we devoted to it. It is a dazzling new capital bursting with pride, and as we found out, much more.

Carpets and
Whirling Dervishes

TRADITIONAL ISLAMIC RELIGIOUS PRACTICE encourages women to cover their heads. As we travel around Turkey it is interesting to observe how both the variety of materials, and methods of tying these head covers have evolved over hundreds of years. For example, women who live and work in country areas, often outdoors, seem to favor tying their small scarves at the nape of the neck after first pulling it behind their ears. In urban areas a larger scarf is often pulled across the face for more privacy. On the windy plains women's scarves are long and can be totally wrapped around their faces to protect from blowing grit and sand. Fabrics range from basic white and solid colors in light cotton, to festive stripes and prints, to heavy black or brown scarves that cover from head to waist.

It was somber, long brown shawls such as this that signaled we had arrived in the conservative city of Konya, located several hours by car south of Ankara. Eight hundred years ago Konya was the capital of the Seljuk empire, but its history begins in prehistoric times. Today it is home to the highly religious sect of the Mevlevi, known to us as whirling dervishes. Its famous mosques and seminaries (medrese), and the presence over the centuries of so many wise teachers of a highly conservative and mystical sect of Islam, have lent the city a serious and quiet air. A large percentage of the women are completely shrouded from head to feet.

Many pilgrims come to Konya to pay their respects and pray at the tomb of Mevlana, who died in 1273. He was the whirling dervishes' founder and most well-known teacher. The sect's famous spinning dance of religious ecstasy is now only performed once a year, but we had come to ancient Konya to see its birthplace.

We also knew Konya to be a center for buying and selling the beautiful carpets made in the region. In each part of the Middle East—Iraq, Iran, Turkey—where hand-tied carpets are made, different patterns have evolved. They are often symbolic, unique to each nomadic group, and have greatly changed over the centuries. The variety is staggering, and even the experts disagree on their origin and meaning, but it is possible for laymen to come to some basic understanding of predominant colors and overall pattern structure. Each type has a name and a region in which it originates. We had taken a particular liking to the pattern and colors of a type called Dosemalti, made near Konya. In big cities like Ankara, and especially in Istanbul, there are examples of carpets from every part of Turkey and beyond. In Istanbul we first spotted the kind we wanted to buy. We were looking for a room-sized carpet and hoped the price would be better in a smaller city closer to its source.

But with only two days planned in Turkey's holy city, first we wanted to visit the great mosque complex of the dervishes and some of the other sights in town. Konya is situated in a fertile oasis, and so its history goes back in mythology and scientific accounts for nine thousand years. In the center of Konya there is an improbably high hill, today covered by a park, which archaeologists have discovered to be the debris mound (called a tell or huyuk) of earlier civilizations on the site. There was a Hittite city, and a Greek settlement called Ikonion here, and later, in the 1st century AD Saint Paul preached in the then Roman city of Claudiconium. After Arab invasions a thousand years ago it was again renamed and became the great secular and religious site it remains today. We walked over the hill and through the park, past a mosque and medrese, and toward the great complex of the Mevlevi mosque. One enters through a gate into a large cloister or courtyard. To the right and left are the former rooms of the students and teachers, and across are the worship and dancing rooms of the sect. Since 1925, at the time of the formation of the republic, the complex has been a museum, but this in no way has dampened the religious fervor of the visitors. This shrine is a special pilgrimage point for devout Moslem women. There were many there, dressed in white, and all were modestly covered from head to foot.

Inside are the rooms containing the coffins of Mevlana and the important teachers who followed him in the past. Every surface shines in the light of votive lamps and candelabra. Cloths embroidered with gold calligraphy are draped over each coffin, and every square inch of wall is covered with elaborate gold patterns. Solemn and mournful music plays in the background. The women press forward to the gates, making pulling motions with their hands across their faces, murmuring prayers. We walked through quietly, not wishing to disturb them, and looked at the incredible richness of detail around us.

In another room, one can visit exhibits of Arabic calligraphy. The Korans there more than rival the illuminated manuscripts of the European Middle Ages. They are meticulously magnificent, true works of art in every way.

Back across the courtyard is an exhibit of extraordinary antique carpets. Many were saved from the damp floors of mosques, having been placed there in layers over the centuries as gifts from the devout. Most are in fragments, their fragile fibers nearly rotted through. Several are large, but many more are prayer rugs, with the characteristic center pattern which is placed to point towards Mecca. These rooms were of particular interest to us and we looked closely at the old patterns and colors.

The complex at Konya was created as a monastery for the Mevlevi, and several small rooms have been set up to show visitors what student bedrooms looked like. They are tiny and sparse, as one might expect, containing only cots, chairs, and writing desks. Over the centuries generations of devoted followers have occupied them during their quest for enlightenment, which was to be achieved by doing a hypnotic whirling dance.

In the late afternoon we left the Mevlevi mosque and strolled the other parts of the town. Konya is a serious place, and we felt that a lot of the lighthearted hustle and bustle of other Turkish towns was definitely missing. That night we found that this atmosphere extended to their restaurants, too. They seemed serviceable and somewhat utilitarian. Konya is a "dry" city, with no alcoholic beverages for sale, so a glass of wine with the evening meal is not possible. Despite the restrictions our meal of cacik, vegetable dolmas, and shepherd's salad was enjoyable, and after dark we walked along the brightly lit main street past many carpet stores. One must be careful about stopping in shops, as it is sometimes hard to break away from the enthusiastic owners. It took several hours to make the rounds and see what was available. We could have floated home on all the tea that was offered, and we did see a few carpets that caught our eye.

In one shop below street level, a bundle of electric wires draped overhead began to spark and sputter, and we were plunged into darkness. Without missing a word, the owner lit candles, and wanted to continue talking. We beat a hasty retreat, and promised to return later, which we did.

The next day we again trekked the length of the long avenue, this time going back only to selected shops. One had a Dosemalti displayed in the window, a beautiful and subtly colored carpet with long warp fringe at the end. We really loved that particular one, but needed to be clever bargainers to get it at an appropriate price. We knew the ritual by now, and knew that we would ultimately pay fifty to sixty percent of that first price if we were skillful. The process took several hours, and we left the store twice to compare at other places. At last the gap began to narrow, both in price and our decision making. One more cup of tea for everyone and the purchase was made. The carpet was tightly rolled, wrapped, and tied, and a boy was dispatched to carry it back to our hotel. A week later, back in Istanbul, we bought a large second-hand suitcase from a street vendor, packed our carpet in it, and carried it home.

The next day we left somber Konya, with its prehistoric huyuk, its devout and modest women, its long and ancient history, and its beautiful shrine. But on our living room floor is a stunning reminder of our visit there.

More Istanbul

L IKE EVERY GREAT CITY, Istanbul reveals itself in layers, slowly over time. The way to savor a city as complex as this is to return again, and yet again; each time discovering something new, or revisiting an old find. Once, years ago, we met a couple in Rome, both teachers like ourselves, who told us that this was their seventeenth consecutive summer-long visit there. When we asked them if they thought they might be growing tired of the same sights, they looked puzzled. Now we understand.

It's difficult to list our favorite places in Istanbul; certainly the small neighborhoods, the public markets, the busy waterfront, and the surrounding hills with the wonderful views. But there are a few places that are so unique they would make anyone's list. They are the Eiffel Towers of Istanbul. Sometimes the most visited places really are the best.

Topkapi Palace sits on a promontory between the Sea of Marmara and the Golden Horn. It was the center of the Ottoman Empire for four hundred years, and into it poured riches from taxes and tribute. Here the reigning sultan and his court—wives, slaves, teachers, government officials—up to four thousand people, lived in a large walled village of pavilions, offices, harems, kitchens, and great halls. Topkapi was the center of government, family life, and religion for the empire. Begun in the 15th century, and added to by each sultan, it has grown to cover almost two hundred acres.

The palace was but a short walk from our hotel, and we started out early one morning to pay it a visit. Thousands tour the grounds daily, and as we walked through the main gate, we looked across the large open courtyard to see crowds forming already. We bought passes and were assigned a group number. The brief wait affords a measure of crowd control, and once inside we did not feel crowded or rushed. One or two areas were closed. We were told that restoration is constant, and parts of the harem would not be accessible that day. There was so much else to see that it hardly seemed to matter.

We walked through beautiful outdoor pavilions with rich, ornate rooms and surrounding gardens. It was in these outdoor spaces that much of palace life took place. Many areas are enhanced with views of the water, and are quite open and expansive.

Off to the right we found the palace kitchen. It is actually a series of specialized smaller kitchens—baking, grilling, vegetable preparation, soups—that fed thousands of people daily. It was generally clear what type of food was prepared in each area. Enormous cauldrons, wok-like pans over fire pits, rows of smaller saucepans hanging overhead, and great hooks for meat were still in place in the simple stone rooms.

Nearby is the harem area, with only a fraction of its hundreds of small rooms open, and then only with a guide. We saw rooms for the harem's slaves and guards, for the sultan's mother, for his chief wives, and for the rearing of the next sultan. They ranged from opulent to depressing depending on the intended occupant. Actually we found that most of the harem was a claustrophobic warren of rooms. In contrast, the sultan's own rooms were rich with beautiful detail, as befitted his station. We were surprised though, to find his bed so low it appeared to be on the floor.

Much of present day Topkapi houses a museum of the treasures that poured in over the centuries. It was here, more than on our tour of the various parts of the palace grounds, that we understood most clearly what life in the palace must have been like. Rooms full of embroidered garments, gold tea sets, jade and porcelain vases, and magnificent jewelry attest to the wealth of the Ottomans. The simplest household items were unbelievably rich. Famous jewels such as the Spoonmaker's Diamond and the sword featured in the film *Top-kapi* are here. In other rooms are displays of precious Islamic artifacts and calligraphy.

It was growing late. Our visit had lasted nearly the entire day. We stopped on our way out of the gates for a refreshing fruit ice from a vendor. Sherbet, in a more liquid form, originated in Turkey, traveling west into Europe at a later date to become the frozen confection we are familiar with. Touring Topkapi had been exhausting but rewarding, and we decided that a visit to Sancta Sophia and the Blue Mosque deserved a day of its own.

One of the greatest buildings in the world is right across from Topkapi. First constructed as a church, then converted to a mosque, and finally to a museum, Sancta Sophia is truly staggering. Built in 500 AD by Justinian, it is an architectural wonder. Its great dome measures over one hundred feet in diameter, almost two hundred feet from floor to top, and has no visible support beyond its walls. Walking into this incredible space in the 20th century is awe inspiring; we could not begin to imagine what someone fifteen hundred years ago must have felt. It was the greatest Christian basilica of the day and is hardly rivaled today. Lit then by thousands of oil lamps, its great interior shone with glittering gold mosaics. Today the fine dust of centuries hangs suspended in the air, creating a subtle haze. We walked from the great dome area into the outer galleries, and finally up some stairs to the upper galleries that encircle the base of the dome itself. It was from there that we had the best views and the truest sense of size. Here too, we were able to see, close up, the few remaining mosaics. Destroyed, repaired, and covered repeatedly over time by Christians and Moslems alike, it is a miracle that any remain. It was, in fact, the plaster cover applied by Moslems when Sancta Sophia became a mosque that saved a few examples. Forgotten, then rediscovered and restored for the museum that Sancta Sophia is today, they are exquisite examples of Byzantine art.

Facing Sancta Sophia, across a road and garden, is the great mosque of Sultan Ahmet. Although over a thousand years separate the two, the strong architectural influence of Sancta Sophia is evident here, and in several other great mosques in Istanbul. It appears that once the Byzantine church became a mosque, and minarets were added, all future mosque building in the city followed the Byzantine architectural cues.

We walked to the mosque of Sultan Ahmet, best known as the Blue Mosque, and entered its great gate. Before us was a large courtyard, and, in the center, a fountain. Men were washing their hands and faces as required before entering the mosque for their daily prayers. Non-Moslem visitors are allowed inside to see the beauty of the interior, but we needed to remove our shoes, and wrap bare legs, arms, and heads with the large cloths provided.

Inside, the great domed space is covered with blue and gold calligraphy. Underfoot lay hundreds of carpets, stacked in additional layers with each pious donation. A small railed-off area to the side is designated for the white-clad women worshippers, and visitors are only allowed behind a railing near the back. The vast remaining areas were filled with Moslem men, facing toward Mecca and kneeling in prayer. We were greatly moved by the tranquillity of this beautiful and pious setting. Over the next days we went on to visit several other great mosques, all built between the 15th and 17th centuries, after the conquest of Byzantium by the Ottomans. Each is beautiful in its own way, and each is well worth visiting.

Near the Blue Mosque, and discovered by us quite by accident one day, is a museum of traditional Turkish and Islamic handicrafts. Housed in a five hundred year old private mansion, its wonderful displays, labeled in Turkish and English, have a kind of immediacy that teaches very well. The materials and processes for gathering, spinning, dying, weaving and tying carpets and kilims are laid out step by step. There are recreations of homes from village life, nomadic tents from several areas and grander Ottoman rooms. Because the making of carpets is women's work, it was gratifying to see a museum that took pains to emphasize their important cultural and economic roles, in a society which often appears to keep them hidden. This museum was a jewel for us, helping to clarify so much we had seen by chance in the Turkish countryside.

There are so many more places to go and things to see than the few mentioned in the three chapters on Istanbul and the Bosporus. One tourist-style map we use lists eighty-six different destinations—mosques, monuments, museums, parks, bazaars, fortifications—within the city. Some are quiet, some grand, some unusual and some amazing.

There is one sight that is all of that and more, and it lay underground just a block from our hotel. We had passed a small sign reading "Roman Cistern" every day. Finally, curiosity drove us to pay a small fee, enter a door and descend into a cavernous and dim nether world. Roman style arches supported by a forest of columns held the unseen city safely above our heads. Each of the hundreds of columns descends into an absolutely still black lake. Stretching as far as we could see into the darkness, punctuated occasionally by discreet lights for our benefit, this strange place was the vast underground water storage area for the Roman city of Constantinople. It was built by Justinian, and today's visitor uses catwalks suspended above the water. It is all eerily beautiful, each column and arch perfectly mirrored in the dark water.

We emerged, blinking in the bright sun, from our underground wanderings. Somehow, our thoughts seem to never be too far from the wonderful Turkish food, and tonight we planned to cross over Galata bridge, and walk up the hill into the new city. There, an area called the Flower Passage is full of small restaurants. Several in particular specialize in fresh fish, and one of those would be our goal, at the end of another magical day in Turkey.

Roman columns in a hot spring, Pamukkale, Turkey

Ephesus, Turkey

Rural road, northern Turkey

Country market, Turkey

Amasra, Turkey

Schoolgirls, Gumushane, Turkey

Roman statue, Aphrodisias, Turkey

Sancta Sophia, Istanbul

Blue Mosque, Istanbul

Ottoman tombstones

Preparing doner kebab

Pamukkale, Turkey

TASTES
OF TURKEY

The Cuisine of Turkey

THE DISCOVERY OF WHAT OTHER CULTURES create with their food, and how cuisines are developed using familiar and sometimes not-so-familiar ingredients, is a constant source of fascination to us. It is surely one of the motivations for our visits to many areas of the world, and we hope that the following recipes will stir the traveler in you, too.

In the past twenty years, Americans have rediscovered how to love good food. This new awakening to the pleasures of fresh ingredients, and the inventive use of a variety of herbs and spices, marries well with an investigation of Turkish recipes. Here is a cuisine that is naturally fresh (Turkey produces all of its own food), nutritious and balanced, easy to prepare, and easy to like. It is complex, yet there is no need to cultivate a palette for extreme new tastes. It is remarkably uniform throughout the country, having been developed and codified centuries ago in the great kitchens of the Ottoman palaces. Later, the recipes became known and prepared, albeit on a simpler scale, by the general population, and today, meals taken both inside and outside the home are virtually identical. Because of the high standards of restaurant cooking, it is possible to eat the best of Turkish cuisine in clean, inexpensive establishments throughout Turkey.

As always, a cuisine must be considered in its context—the climate, prosperity, geography, and perhaps religious customs of a culture. These and other factors contribute to its development. In the case of Turkey, some of the earliest recipes were developed by nomads and peasants, and involved skewered meats (sis kebab) for grilling, food wrapped in small packages (borek), and one-dish meals. Easy to prepare, easy to carry, with few utensils needed, these clearly fit their lifestyle.

Later, when the Ottomans elaborated on and refined recipes, they began borrowing ingredients such as olive oil, fish, and new varieties of fruits and vegetables from the west. Fresh herbs grew naturally, and spices were brought to them by sea and caravan from the east. Today, the land is heavily cultivated, and hundreds of ingredients, such as shoppers can find in the so-called Egyptian Bazaar in Istanbul or in any small town market, combine to create their uniquely delicious smells and tastes. Indeed, many believe that the three greatest cuisines of the world are French, Chinese, and Turkish.

Although the ingredients seem endless, lamb is the most popular meat, with chicken and seafood of all kinds also popular. Cooking is done in butter or olive oil, and rice is the most common grain. Their dairy products include soft cheeses, made with sheep or cow milk, and rich creamy yogurt. Tomatoes, eggplant, peppers, zucchini, onions, cucumbers, potatoes, green beans, and artichokes are among the most frequently enjoyed vegetables. Their fresh breads are wonderful, their desserts often intensely sweet. Raisins, pistachios, walnuts, and hazelnuts are combined with savory foods as often as with sweets. Dried beans, lentils, and olives, and favorite fruits such as melons, cherries, figs, grapes, peaches, and apricots are served everywhere. Dominant flavors include fresh lemon juice, mint, parsley, oregano, dill, flavorful honey, allspice, and cinnamon.

Tea with lemon or sugar is the beverage of hospitality and business transactions; their coffee is served in tiny cups—sweet, thick, and dark. A typical breakfast includes bread, olives, yogurt, and soft cheese, perhaps honey and fresh melon. Sherbet, as a fruit drink, started here, as did the coffee house or café before traveling west to Europe in the 16th century.

To cook as they do in Turkey, start the meal with many small snacks called meze, and raki, an anise flavored liqueur. Leave out any pork, always use fresh herbs, serve each dish separately, go easy on the alcohol, and end the meal with fresh fruit, strong coffee, and perhaps a small sweet.

To construct a typical formal menu, choose several meze, one meat or fish dish, one pilav or rice dish, one vegetable dish, and one confection. Lighter meals of soup and bread, or a kebab and salad, make a fine lunch. Turkish cooks take pride in attractively arranged and garnished platters of food. Set your table with a centerpiece of candles and fruit.

It is a happy feature of the Turkish cuisine that the vast majority of dishes can be prepared ahead, so you can sit back and relax at mealtime and enjoy the praise of your guests!

Miscellaneous Notes
and Cooking Tips

- Many recipes in this book have had the fats and oils reduced to bring them more into line with modern calorie-conscious tastes. But in the matter of yogurt, there can be no compromise. For the most authentic Turkish taste, select rich full-fat yogurt of the best quality.

- Use the best canned beef and chicken stock when called for. Price is a good indicator. Do not use bouillon cubes or reconstituted stock. To degrease, refrigerate the unopened cans, and when opened, the fat will be sitting on the top in several globules. Pick off with a small slotted spoon.

- Although canned tomatoes are better than supermarket fresh ones for use in cooking during winter, summer home-grown or farmer's market tomatoes are great when you can get them. The cans come in 14-ounce and 28-ounce sizes.

- Imported black calamata olives are infinitely more tasty than canned, pitted "American style" olives. Use them when olives are called for.

- Use fresh herbs, lemon juice, onions, and garlic in all recipes unless specifically stated otherwise. Bottled or dried versions are just not the same.

- A blender or food processor makes life easier in any kitchen and is indispensable in many recipes in this book.

- Buy a good medium-sized stainless wire whisk. It is extremely useful for mixing ingredients quickly and more thoroughly than a spoon.

- One lemon equals approximately 4 tablespoons of juice; a half lemon equals 2 tablespoons. Either way of measuring is fine in all of the recipes that call for lemon in this book. Always use fresh lemon juice.

- Pide bread is very similar to the packaged pita or pocket bread sold in most supermarkets and Middle Eastern bakeries. It is used in Turkey in the same way as a Mexican flour tortilla is—that is, as a "dish" or wrap for foods.

- Grilling, a popular cooking method for vegetables, meat, and fish in Turkey, is always done there on a real charcoal fire. Nothing substitutes for the flavor imparted by the glowing red-orange coals. If possible, use the real thing rather than gas or electric grills or ovens. The flavor of the kebabs, whether meat or fish, will be greatly improved.

- In Turkey, grilled kebabs are never left on their skewers when they are served. They are slid off onto individual plates and presented to the diner. Oiling the skewers before grilling helps.

- Choose the best quality extra virgin olive oil for all Turkish, as well as Mediterranean and Middle Eastern, cuisine. Do not use bland olive oil "blends" or less than the finest grade.

- Phyllo and strudel dough are the same thing. It can be purchased frozen in good supermarkets and specialty shops, and keeps very well if tightly wrapped in the freezer. Only remove what is needed, and allow to thaw overnight, also well wrapped, in the refrigerator. It must be protected from drying out under plastic wrap even as you are using it.

- The word "pilav" refers to the preparation of rice. It is rice cooked with stock. Long grain white rice or basmati rice are the most appropriate for all pilav recipes. Brown rice is seldom seen in Turkish cooking. Never use instant rice.

MEZE

A SURE SIGN OF A GOOD HOSTESS or a fine restaurant in Turkey is the variety and number of different meze served before dinner. These snacks or hors d'oeuvres are, typically, savory finger foods, and are accompanied by the national drink, an anise flavored liquor called raki. Occasionally they are served by themselves at a kind of sit down cocktail party called a raki table. Of course, individual meze can be eaten alone or as part of a light lunch.

To begin your Turkish meal, set out dishes of sliced feta cheese, green and black olives, and prepare several hot or cold selections from among the meze recipes.

Cheese and Meat Borek

There are many varieties of borek in Turkey. They are delectable little packages of phyllo pastry, typically filled with meat or cheese, then rolled and baked. Phyllo sheets can be purchased frozen in most supermarkets and specialty food shops.

Cheese filling:

> ¾ pound feta cheese
> 1 egg
> ½ cup chopped fresh parsley
> 2 tablespoons chopped fresh dill

Mash the feta cheese and mix thoroughly with the egg, or whirl both in a food processor for a few seconds.

Add the parsley and dill.

Set aside.

Meat Filling:

> ¾ pound ground meat (lamb or beef)
> 1 medium onion, minced
> 1 beaten egg
> ½ cup chopped fresh parsley
> salt and pepper to taste

In a skillet, break up the meat and brown with the onion. Remove from the heat, drain off any fat, and allow to cool.

Add the egg, parsley, salt, and pepper.

Set aside.

Phyllo pastry:

> 1 pound package frozen phyllo sheets (will be enough for both cheese and meat recipes)
> 1 stick melted butter (more as needed)
> (pastry brush)

Allow the package to defrost naturally in the refrigerator overnight. Unwrap carefully. Working quickly, cut through all of the sheets to create 60 to 80 3 x 12 inch pieces. Stack the pieces and cover with plastic wrap. Do not allow phyllo sheets to dry out.

To make the cheese borek:

Remove one sheet of phyllo from under the wrap, brush lightly with melted butter. Place one rounded teaspoon of cheese mix 1 inch from the short end. Start to roll firmly over the cheese from this end, folding in ½ inch from each side as you go. Roll to the end. It should look like a cigarette. (They are called Sigara Borek in Turkey!)

Place, seam side down, on a lightly greased baking sheet. Make more rolls in the same manner until the cheese mix is used up. Brush the tops of all the borek with additional butter.

Bake in a 350° oven for 20 to 25 minutes, or until golden. Makes 30 to 40 borek.

To make the meat borek:

Traditionally these are folded into triangular packages. To make this type of fold, place one rounded teaspoon of the meat mix 1 inch from the short end of a lightly buttered phyllo sheet. Fold over both long sides evenly onto the meat so that now the folded sheet is 1 inch wide by 12 inches long.

Next, fold the left bottom corner over the meat and across to the right edge to create a small triangle.

Continue folding the triangle up along the length of the phyllo sheet, exactly as one would fold a flag, wrapping the meat inside.

Place the borek close together on a lightly greased baking sheet. Brush all borek with additional butter.

Bake in a 350° oven for 20 to 25 minutes, or until golden. Makes 30 to 40 borek.

Stuffed Grape Leaves

The Turkish people are very fond of stuffing all manner of ingredients into a great variety of vegetable "containers." These dishes are called dolmas. Although most are served as main or side dishes, the following well-known dolma is served as a snack or meze.

            1 bottle of preserved grape leaves
          ¼ cup olive oil
            1 large onion, minced
          ¾ cup uncooked rice
          ½ cup pine nuts
          ½ cup currants
            1 cup chicken stock
            1 tablespoon chopped fresh dill
            1 tablespoon chopped fresh parsley
          ¼ teaspoon ground allspice
          ¼ teaspoon ground cinnamon
            salt and pepper to taste
            2 lemons
            yogurt (optional)

Separate, rinse, and carefully dry the grape leaves. Cut off any tough stem portions. Set aside.

In a skillet with a tight-fitting lid, heat the oil, sauté the onion, and add the rice, pine nuts, and currants. Continue to sauté until the rice is glazed.

Add the stock, dill, parsley, allspice, cinnamon, salt, and pepper.

Lower the heat, cover the skillet, and allow all to simmer for fifteen minutes. Remove from the heat, uncover, and allow to cool.

Place the first grape leaf, shiny side down, on a work surface. Place one tablespoon or more (depending on the size of the leaf) of the rice mixture at the stem end, fold in the edges, and roll firmly to make a secure package.

Continue until all of the rice mix and leaves are used. Use some flat leaves to line the bottom of a broad lidded pot. Wedge the rolled leaf and rice mix packages in tightly along the bottom of the pot. If it is necessary to create a second layer, place several additional flat leaves between the layers.

Press a heavy inverted plate over the grape leaf packages to prevent over-expansion and movement while they cook.

Squeeze the juice from one lemon and add it, plus enough water to cover the plate, to the pot. Cover and simmer for forty minutes.

Uncover the pot. Allow all to cool a bit, then carefully lift out the packages with a slotted spoon. Allow them to drain and cool.

Arrange the dolmas on a platter with lemon slices, and, if desired, serve with unflavored yogurt for dipping. Serve at room temperature or chilled.

White Cheese Purée

This is an excellent spicy dip or spread for crackers or small slices of bread.

⅓ pound feta cheese
3 rounded tablespoons unflavored yogurt
1 clove garlic, minced
⅛ teaspoon cayenne pepper
1 tablespoon olive oil
2 tablespoons fresh parsley, minced

Mash the feta cheese and mix with all other ingredients ...

or

Whirl all ingredients, except the parsley, in a food processor until smooth. Add parsley.

Chill. This is tastier if made a day ahead.

Mashed Chickpeas

Mashed chickpeas prepared this way is called hummus. It is used as a dip or spread on crackers, warm pide bread, or raw vegetables. It is a snap to make in a blender or food processor, but can be mashed and mixed by hand.

    1 15-ounce can of chickpeas, drained
   ¾ cup tahini (see note with Eggplant Spread recipe)
   ¾ cup lemon juice (3 lemons)
   3 cloves garlic, minced
      salt and pepper to taste
      garnishes of lemon, black calamata olives,
      parsley if desired

Place the chickpeas, tahini, lemon juice, garlic, salt, and pepper in a blender or food processor. Blend for a few seconds to form a smooth paste. Check and adjust salt and pepper.

Mound into a serving dish, garnish with lemon slices, olives, and chopped parsley. Chill. Serve at room temperature.

White Beans Plaki

"Plaki" refers to preparing various vegetables with tomatoes, onions, garlic, and olive oil, and serving them cold. Bean dishes are very common in a meze assortment and can be prepared ahead.

¼ cup olive oil
1 medium onion, chopped
2 cloves garlic, minced
1 large ripe tomato, chopped
1 medium carrot, peeled and diced
1 medium potato, peeled and diced
1 stalk celery, thinly sliced
1 cup canned chicken stock
2 15-ounce cans of Great Northern beans,
    or other white beans, drained
    salt and pepper to taste
2 tablespoons lemon juice (½ lemon)
1 tablespoon fresh parsley, minced

Heat the olive oil in a deep saucepot. Lightly brown the onion and garlic. Add tomato, carrot, potato, and celery. Stir and sauté for several more minutes. Add the stock and simmer for ten minutes.

Add the drained beans, salt, pepper, and lemon juice. Slowly simmer for an additional 10 minutes, or until vegetables are tender. Do not let the stock evaporate. Add a bit more stock (or water) if necessary.

Remove from the heat. Transfer to a serving bowl. Allow to cool. Serve at room temperature, sprinkled with parsley.

Green Bean Salad

This refreshing dish can, of course, be served as a vegetable or salad with a meal, but it is often found on a raki table as a meze.

> 1 pound fresh string beans
> 3 tablespoons olive oil
> 1 onion, chopped
> 1 ripe tomato, chopped
>   salt and pepper to taste
> ½ cup water
> 2 tablespoons lemon juice (½ lemon)
> ¼ cup fresh parsley, minced

Remove stems from the beans, wash and cut into 1 inch pieces.

Heat oil in a lidded saucepan. Sauté onion for several minutes, then add tomato and beans. Continue to toss and sauté for several minutes, then add salt, pepper, and water.

Cover and simmer for 15 minutes, or until beans are tender. The water should have evaporated and be nearly gone.

Remove from the heat, check seasonings, add lemon juice, and chill.

Serve at room temperature sprinkled with parsley.

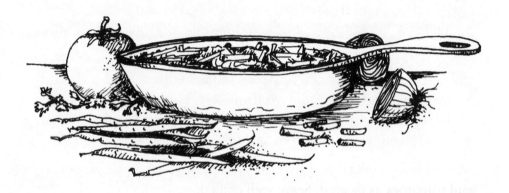

Eggplant Spread

This classic is easy to prepare with a blender or food processor. The flavor improves by making one or two days ahead. Tahini, which is sesame seed butter, can be purchased in cans or jars in specialty groceries or stores that carry Middle Eastern food ingredients. Once opened, it keeps a long time refrigerated and is used in several recipes in this book. The oil will separate and needs to be mixed back in at room temperature.

1 medium eggplant
4 tablespoons lemon juice (1 lemon)
4 tablespoon tahini
2 or 3 garlic cloves, minced
1 tablespoon olive oil
¼ teaspoon salt
¼ cup fresh parsley, minced

garnishes:

parsley
lemon slices
black calamata olives
tomato wedges

First the eggplant needs to be roasted in its skin. Do this over a charcoal fire, right over the flames on a stovetop, or under a broiler. Turn frequently until the skin is blackened and the eggplant is quite soft. Allow to cool.

Cut open the eggplant and scoop all the flesh out into a bowl. Add lemon juice, tahini, garlic, olive oil and salt. Mash and mix all ingredients together, or place all above ingredients into a blender or food processor, and whirl until smooth. Stir in the minced parsley.

Mound onto a plate, and garnish with parsley, lemon slices, olives, and tomatoes as desired. Serve well chilled.

Potato Balls

If made ahead, these reheat nicely on a cookie sheet placed in a hot oven for a few minutes.

4 medium potatoes
2 eggs
½ cup grated Parmesan or Romano cheese
¼ teaspoon onion powder
⅛ teaspoon garlic powder
   salt and pepper to taste
1 egg, beaten
1 cup dry bread crumbs
1 cup vegetable oil for frying
   Yogurt Sauce, page 190

Boil potatoes in their skins until tender. Drain, cool and peel.

Place potatoes, eggs, cheese, onion and garlic powders, salt, and pepper in a food processor to purée, or mash above ingredients together in a bowl until smooth.

Roll potato mix into 1 inch balls, dip in beaten egg, then coat with bread crumbs.

Heat the oil in a large skillet, and fry the potato balls until golden. Drain on paper towels.

Serve with Yogurt Sauce.

Fried Eggplant with Two Sauces

Eggplant prepared this way is very popular in Turkey, especially when served as an appetizer or meze. Eggplant has the ability to act as a sponge for oil, so it is best to use the following modifications to cut down on the calories in frying.

> 1 large eggplant
> salt
> olive oil for frying
> Yogurt Sauce, page 190
> Tomato Sauce, page 190

After cutting the stem off, slice the eggplant into ⅓ inch round slices. Liberally salt both sides of each round, and allow to rest for 30 minutes on paper towels. Rinse off the salt and pat each slice very dry with additional paper towels.

Preheat a large skillet and pour only 1 or 2 tablespoons of oil into the bottom. Spread the oil around, and place in to fry as many rounds of eggplant that will fit in one layer. After they begin to color, remove them to a plate and put an additional 1 or 2 tablespoons of oil into the skillet. Turn the slices, uncooked side down, and fry that side until golden.

Continue until all slices are fried. You must limit the oil they are allowed to soak up or they would become quite soggy with it.

An alternate method: Brush each eggplant slice on both sides with a pastry brush dipped in olive oil. Place on a cookie sheet, and brown first on one side, then the other, under a hot broiler.

Set out finished eggplant slices in one layer on a large platter lined with paper towels.

Prepare Yogurt Sauce and Tomato Sauce. Refrigerate the eggplant and the two sauces for several hours, covered.

At serving time, bring all to room temperature. Remove the paper towels. Spread half the slices with Yogurt Sauce, and the remaining slices with Tomato Sauce.

Zucchini Fritters

These savory fritters can be served as a side dish with a meal, too. Choose small young zucchini as large ones contain too much water to make this recipe successfully.

> 5 small zucchini
> 3 eggs, beaten
> 1 medium onion, minced
> ¼ cup fresh dill, chopped
> ¼ cup fresh mint, chopped
> ½ cup fresh parsley, chopped
> ¼ cup grated Parmesan cheese
> ¼ cup grated Swiss-type cheese
> ⅛ teaspoon cayenne pepper
>   salt to taste
> 1 cup flour
> 1 cup vegetable oil for frying
>   Yogurt Sauce, page 190

Wash, dry, and grate zucchini into a bowl. Add eggs, onion, dill, mint, parsley, cheeses, cayenne pepper, and salt. Mix well. Add flour and mix until it is just incorporated.

Heat oil until quite hot in a large skillet. Drop zucchini mix, 1 tablespoon at a time, into the oil. Do not let them touch. Turn once, fry until golden. Fry additional batches until all have been done. Drain on paper towels.

Serve hot with Yogurt Sauce.

Fried Cauliflower

This is a nice way to prepare an often mundane and underappreciated vegetable.

    salt
    1 cauliflower
    1 cup flour
    3 eggs, beaten
    1½ cups grated Parmesan cheese
    1 cup vegetable oil for frying
    Yogurt Sauce, page 190

Trim the cauliflower into bite-sized pieces. Put a large deep pot of well salted water on to boil. When it is boiling, drop in the cauliflower pieces. Boil them for a few minutes, until they begin to soften. Drain and allow to cool on a large flat platter.

Toss the cool cauliflower pieces lightly in the flour. Shake off excess flour. Dip each piece in the beaten eggs, then in the grated cheese.

Heat the oil in a large skillet and gently fry the pieces, turning them to each side as best you can. Drain on paper towels.

Serve hot with Yogurt Sauce.

Fried Carrots

To American tastes, carrots are somewhat of an unusual vegetable to prepare this way, but they often show up on a raki table as a meze in Turkey.

    4 or 5 large carrots
    1 teaspoon salt
    1 egg, beaten
    1 cup flour
    1 cup vegetable oil for frying
      salt and pepper
      Yogurt Sauce, page 190
      fresh dill

Choose carrots with a large diameter. Peel and cut into ¼ inch round slices.

Place slices in a large pot of boiling water with the salt. Boil until tender but not soft. Drain and cool.

Dip each slice in egg, then flour to coat. Heat oil in a large skillet. Fry on each side until golden. Drain on paper towels.

Serve with a bowl of Yogurt Sauce for dipping. Garnish with dill.

Liver Tidbits

A proper meze assortment should include both hot and cold dishes. This quick and easy snack is a popular hot choice. Every preparation step up to the actual frying can be done before the guests arrive.

> 1 pound calf liver
> ¼ teaspoon cayenne pepper
> 1 tablespoon paprika
> ½ cup flour
> ½ teaspoon salt
> ¾ cup olive oil
> 1 large onion, finely sliced into rings
> ¼ cup fresh parsley, minced

Cut the liver into ½ inch cubes.

Mix pepper, paprika, flour, and salt together in a plastic bag large enough to hold the liver cubes. Put the cubes in the bag, seal the top, and gently shake until all the liver pieces are separately and evenly coated with the flour mix. Turn the pieces out into a strainer and shake to remove any excess flour.

Heat the oil in a large skillet until very hot. Sauté the cubes quickly on all sides in the oil. Three to four minutes total is enough; do not overcook. With a slotted spoon scoop out onto paper towels to drain for a moment, then transfer the liver cubes to their serving dish. Top with raw onion rings and parsley. Serve at once with small forks or toothpicks.

Fried Mussels

Fried mussels like these are a common street vendor food in coastal areas of Turkey, sold three or four to a wooden skewer. At home, they (and Stuffed Mussels—Fish section) are served as hors d'oeuvres. These are always presented with Tarator Sauce.

> 40 mussels
> 2 eggs
> ¼ teaspoon salt
> 1 cup flour
> 1 cup olive oil
>   Tarator Sauce, page 193
>   lettuce leaves, lemon wedges

Scrub mussels in running water; do not soak. Pull off beard and any bits of debris on the outside of the shell.

Place ½ inch of water in a large lidded pot. Bring to a boil. Put in 10 mussels at a time. Cover for 30 seconds. They should have started to open, if not give them another 30 seconds in the hot steam. Remove from the pot with a slotted spoon. Do the next 3 batches of 10 mussels in the same way.

When they have cooled, take the mussels out of the half opened shells. Throw away the shells. Discard any mussels that did not start to open after 1 minute in the hot water and steam.

In a small bowl, beat the eggs with the salt. Dip each mussel in the eggs, then carefully roll each mussel in the flour. Set aside on a plate to dry for a few minutes so they won't spatter when fried.

Heat the oil in a skillet until quite hot. Drop the mussels, a few at a time, into the oil, and fry on both sides until golden, about 2 to 3 minutes total. Drain on paper towels.

Make the Tarator Sauce and place a small bowl of it in the center of a platter. Arrange the mussels on a bed of lettuce leaves around the sauce bowl. Place a toothpick in each. Garnish with lemon wedges. Serve hot.

Cocktail Meat "Fingers"

These do not differ much from American style cocktail meatballs, except in the shape.

¾ pound ground beef
1 onion, finely grated, with its juice
2 eggs, beaten
4 tablespoons plain dried bread crumbs
¼ cup fresh parsley, minced
¼ teaspoon ground cumin
   salt and pepper to taste
1 cup flour
1 cup vegetable oil for frying
   mustard

Place the beef, onion and onion juice, eggs, bread crumbs, parsley, cumin, salt, and pepper in a bowl. Knead with hands until very smooth.

Form into 2 inch long finger shapes. Roll in flour.

Heat the oil in a skillet and fry the meat fingers over medium heat until golden.

Insert a toothpick in each, and serve hot, accompanied by mustard for dipping. Makes about 40 fingers.

SOUPS

As IN MOST CUISINES, soups in Turkey can be either delicate or hearty. Not surprisingly, the more delicate or thinner soups serve as a first course in a formal dinner, while the more hearty and filling soups are often served alone or with a salad for lunch.

Several touches, though, make soup eating in Turkey unique. Traditionally, soups here are eaten with wooden spoons, to preserve, it is believed, their purity of taste. And secondly, final ingredients such as lemon, yogurt, and parsley are often added by each diner at the table.

Cold Cucumber and Yogurt Soup

This is an easy and completely traditional Turkish soup. It is a refreshing summertime treat that with a bit more cucumber and a bit less yogurt changes into a salad (see: Cucumber Yogurt Salad, page 174). It is called cacik.

1 large cucumber
¼ teaspoon salt
1 clove garlic, peeled and cut in half
2 cups yogurt
1 tablespoon olive oil
2 tablespoons vinegar
¼ cup fresh dill, chopped
¼ cup fresh mint, chopped
pinch of cayenne pepper

Peel the cucumber and cut lengthwise. Scoop out the seeds by running a spoon down its inside length.

Coarsely grate the cucumber, collecting the pulp and the juice in a bowl. Sprinkle with salt, mix, and let stand a while.

Rub the inside of another bowl with both halves of the garlic clove. Discard the clove.

Mix the yogurt, olive oil, vinegar, dill, mint, and cayenne pepper together in this bowl.

Add the cucumbers and their salty liquid. Mix again. Add more salt and pepper if desired.

Serve thoroughly chilled in individual soup bowls. Serves 4.

Cold Tomato Soup

A perfect summertime soup, easy to prepare, cool and refreshing.

> 1 cup yogurt
> 3 cups canned tomato juice
> 1 tablespoon olive oil
> 2 tablespoons lemon juice
> 2 tablespoons white vinegar
> ½ teaspoon curry powder
>   salt to taste
>   lemon, sliced wafer thin
>   fresh parsley, minced

In a large bowl, stir yogurt until smooth. Using a wire whisk, beat in the tomato juice, olive oil, lemon juice, vinegar, and curry powder. Taste, and add salt if desired.

Chill for several hours.

Ladle into chilled bowls, float a lemon slice on each, and sprinkle with parsley. Serves 4.

Lemon Chicken Soup

An extremely simple soup, this is a favorite in Turkey. It is a perfect first course at a formal dinner, or with borek and other meze at a light summer lunch. Use the best quality chicken stock.

> 5 cups chicken stock
> 2 eggs and 1 egg yolk
> 4 tablespoons lemon juice (1 lemon)
> 2 tablespoons fresh parsley, chopped

In a saucepan, bring the stock to a boil and lower heat.

Beat the eggs, yolk, and lemon juice together well.

Slowly add a cup of hot stock to the egg mix, stirring constantly. Then add this to the large pot of stock, again stirring constantly.

Heat just to the boil, but do not allow to boil.

Serve hot. Sprinkle each serving with chopped parsley. Serves 6.

(Beef) Yogurt Soup 1

The following are two surprising yogurt and stock soups that are each a perfect light start to a large meal. They are similarly quick and easy.

   1 quart good quality canned beef stock
   2 cups yogurt
      salt and pepper to taste
   4 tablespoons butter
   4 tablespoons flour
  ½ clove garlic, minced
      fresh mint, chopped

Mix the beef stock, yogurt, salt, and pepper together in a bowl.

In a large saucepan, melt the butter, add the flour and garlic. Cook for several moments.

With the heat in high, slowly add the beef stock mix, stirring constantly until all comes to a boil. Cook the thickened mix for several minutes.

Serve hot in individual bowls. Pass fresh mint as a garnish. Serves 6.

(Chicken) Yogurt Soup II

1 quart good quality canned chicken stock
⅓ cup white rice
2 cups yogurt
2 eggs
    salt and pepper to taste
    fresh mint, chopped

In a large saucepan, simmer the stock and rice for about 15 minutes, or until the rice is tender. Remove the pot from the heat.

Meanwhile, beat together the yogurt and eggs.

Slowly add the yogurt mix to the hot stock, stirring constantly. When all is stirred in, return the pot to the heat, and bring the soup to just under a boil, stirring constantly. Do not allow to boil.

Serve immediately in individual bowls. Pass chopped mint as a garnish. Serves 6.

Turkish Vegetable Soup

This puréed vegetable soup can be served either hot or cold. It resembles a borsch because of the beets which color it.

> 2 tablespoons butter
> 2 stalks celery, cut in pieces
> 2 carrots, peeled and cut in pieces
> 2 cloves garlic, minced
> 2 onions, chopped
> 6 cups of good quality canned beef stock
> 2 medium potatoes, peeled and cut in pieces
> 1 red sweet pepper, seeded and chopped
> 2 ripe tomatoes, chopped
> ¼ head of cabbage, chopped
> 3 beet roots, scrubbed
> 1 bay leaf
> 2 cups yogurt
> 4 tablespoons lemon juice (1 lemon)
>   salt and pepper to taste
> 1 tablespoon fresh dill, minced
>   fresh parsley, minced

In a large, lidded saucepot, melt the butter and sauté the celery, carrots, garlic, and onions for 4 minutes.

Pour in the stock, and add potatoes, pepper, tomatoes, cabbage, beets, and bay leaf.

Bring to a boil, reduce to a simmer. Cover and cook for 1 hour or until the beets are tender. Take off the heat and allow to cool. Remove the bay leaf and discard. Remove the 3 beets, and when able to handle them, slip their skins off. Cut up the beets and return to the soup.

In a blender or food processor, purée the soup in batches until smooth.

With a wire whisk, add 1½ cups of the yogurt, the lemon juice, salt, pepper, and dill.

Serve hot; or thoroughly chill overnight, and serve cold. Either way, place a dollop of the remaining yogurt, and a sprinkle of parsley on the soup in each individual bowl. Serves 8.

Red Lentil Soup

You may have to hunt a bit for red lentils. Regular brown lentils taste the same and are fine, but nothing can substitute for the beautiful rich yellow color of the soup when made the Turkish way, with red lentils. It is a hearty and nutritious winter soup, and a particular favorite of ours.

>1 cup red lentils
>6 tablespoons butter (divided)
>1 large onion, chopped
>4 cups water
>2 tablespoons flour
>4 cups good quality canned beef stock
>2 eggs
>1 cup milk
>   salt and cayenne pepper to taste
>4 or 5 slices of day-old French or Italian bread
>   fresh parsley, chopped
>   fresh mint, chopped

Wash and pick over the lentils. In a large saucepot, melt 2 tablespoons of the butter and lightly brown the onion. Add the water and lentils. Bring to a boil, reduce heat, and simmer for 30 to 40 minutes, or until the lentils are quite soft. Allow to cool slightly.

In a small saucepan, melt 2 more tablespoons of butter, add the flour, and allow to foam and cook together for 1 minute. Slowly add in 1 cup of the stock, stirring constantly over heat until the mixture thickens.

In a blender or food processor, purée the lentil and water mix until smooth. Return to the large pot, add the remaining 3 cups of stock, and bring to a boil.

Slowly add in the flour and stock mix from the small pot, stirring well. Reduce heat and simmer for five minutes.

In a bowl, beat the eggs and milk together well. Slowly add to the hot soup. Do not allow to boil again.

Add salt and cayenne pepper to taste.

To make croutons: Cut the bread into ½ inch cubes. Melt the last 2 tablespoons of butter in a skillet, and fry the bread cubes on all sides until golden.

Serve the soup hot. Pass garnishes of croutons, parsley, and mint for each person to add as desired. Serves 8.

Wedding Soup

This soup is served at all weddings in Turkey. It is hearty and delicious, perfect as a first course or for lunch.

> 1 pound lamb pieces, trimmed of fat
> 1 carrot, peeled and sliced
> 1 onion, chopped
> 1½ quarts water
>   salt and pepper to taste
> 6 tablespoons butter
> ½ cup flour
> 4 tablespoons lemon juice (1 lemon)
> 3 egg yolks

garnishes:

> 3 tablespoons butter
> 1 tablespoon paprika
> ⅛ teaspoon cayenne pepper

In a large saucepot, combine the lamb, carrot, onion, water, salt, and pepper.

Bring to a boil, cover, and simmer for 1½ hours, or until lamb is quite tender.

Cool a bit, strain off the meat and vegetables, and save the stock. Shred the lamb, discard the vegetables.

In a separate saucepan, melt the 6 tablespoons of butter, and add the flour. Stir and cook for several minutes, then slowly add the stock, whisking constantly until bubbling and smooth.

Add the meat shreds and simmer for 10 minutes.

Beat the lemon juice and egg yolks together in a bowl. Stir in a cup of the hot soup, then slowly add it all to the soup pot, whisking well. Heat but do not allow it to boil.

In a small pot, melt the butter for the garnish. Stir in the paprika and cayenne pepper.

Serve individual hot bowls of soup. Pass the melted butter mix so that each person may add a spoon of it to their soup. Serves 6 to 8.

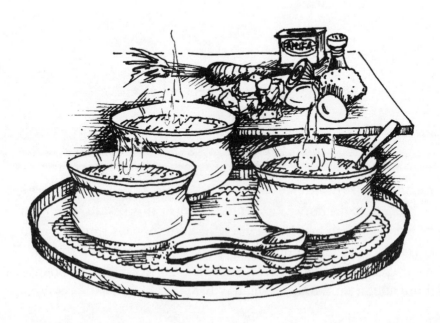

MEAT AND POULTRY

LAMB IS FAR AND AWAY the most popular meat in Turkey. Some veal and beef are consumed, but never pork, as Turkey is a predominantly Islamic nation. Of poultry, chicken is the most common, and several chicken dishes are justifiably famous.

There are two hallmarks of Turkish meat and poultry cuisine. The first is the tendency to cube (kebab), grind, or mince meat into bite-sized pieces before cooking.

Sis means "stick" in Turkish, and many recipes involve threading or wrapping this cubed and ground meat onto sis (skewers). The most familiar, simplest and best of these quintessentially Turkish recipes is sis kebab. Here, small cubes of tender young lamb, marinated in lemon juice and olive oil, are threaded onto skewers and grilled over a hot fire.

The second distinguishing feature of Turkish cuisine is the combining of meat with vegetables in the preparation and cooking stages, so as to combine flavors.

Look through the vegetable section of this book for many additional meat recipes. In Turkey, these meat/vegetable dishes are as frequently served as a main dish, as is meat alone.

One famous Turkish meat recipe that is almost impossible to prepare at home is the doner kebab. Marinated grilled lamb, served on fresh pide bread with spicy yogurt sauce, it is always eaten in small restaurants or standing outside at their street counter grills.

To prepare it, the proprietor begins by marinating many pounds of thinly sliced young lamb the day before. Then these slices, plus lamb fat and ground lamb are layered onto a long heavy skewer. This is fastened vertically in front of banked charcoal fires, where it slowly turns and grills for hours. Succulent thin slices are cut at each customer's request, and either wrapped in flat pide bread for a walking feast, or served flat on a plate inside the restaurant as a light and satisfying meal.

When preparing most of the following recipes, it is possible to substitute tender young veal or beef for the lamb, but a good deal of the typically Turkish taste will be missing.

Grilled Lamb Chops

In Turkey, sheep are said to feast on fresh wild thyme in the fields where they graze. This imparts a subtle flavor to the meat, and the wise cook enhances this taste by marinating lamb chops or roasts in additional fresh thyme.

1 large onion
1 teaspoon salt
2 tablespoons olive oil
1 tablespoon lemon juice
2 tablespoons fresh thyme, chopped
8 lamb chops
fresh parsley, chopped

Grate the onion onto a large deep platter. Mix well with the salt, olive oil, lemon juice, and thyme.

Turn the chops in this marinade until coated, lay out on the platter in the marinade, cover, and refrigerate for several hours. Turn once or twice.

The most genuine taste comes from real charcoal fire, but artificial charcoal grills, wood fires, or even kitchen broilers will do the job. Preheat well. Place the chops close enough to the heat so that in no more than 4 or 5 minutes each side will be seared, but the insides will remain pink.

Serve immediately, garnished with parsley. Serves 4.

Roast Leg of Lamb

Like the preceding recipe for Grilled Lamb Chops, simplicity is best with this succulent meat. Fresh thyme is again an essential ingredient in the marinade.

1 leg of lamb, 5 to 6 pounds
4 tablespoons lemon juice (1 lemon)
1 teaspoon salt
1 teaspoon pepper
1 tablespoon paprika
2 cloves of garlic, minced
2 tablespoons olive oil
2 tablespoons fresh thyme, minced
2 tablespoons yogurt

Trim lamb of most fat.

In a small bowl, mix together all the remaining ingredients.

Place the meat on a rack in a roasting pan, fat side up. Coat the meat completely with marinade. Allow to marinate for 1 hour at room temperature.

Preheat oven to 450°.

Place the meat in the oven, and immediately reduce the heat to 350°. Roast for 24 minutes per pound.

Allow meat to rest out of the oven for 10 minutes after roasting. Slice, and serve with a pilav. Serves 8.

Sultan's Delight

This rather poetically named dish is really a simple lamb stew, made elegant when surrounded by Eggplant Purée. It was created in the Topkapi Palace kitchens.

> 2 pounds of boneless lamb
> 2 tablespoons butter
> 2 medium onions, chopped
> 1 large can of chopped tomatoes (28 ounces)
>   salt and pepper to taste
>   Eggplant Purée, page 194
> ¼ cup fresh parsley, chopped

Remove the visible fat from the lamb and cut into ¾ inch cubes. In a large skillet heat the butter. Add the onions and lamb pieces. Sauté until lightly browned.

Add the tomatoes plus their liquid to the skillet. Add salt and pepper to taste.

Reduce the heat to a simmer, cover, and cook slowly for 1 hour or more, until the meat is tender. Add a bit of water from time to time if needed. The meat should be moist but not swimming in sauce when done.

Serve hot on a platter surrounded by Eggplant Purée and garnish with chopped parsley. Serves 6.

Gardener's Kebab

"Kebab" refers to recipes in which the meat, poultry, or fish is cut into bite-sized cubes before cooking. Stewing, braising, and grilling are possible cooking methods for this cubed meat, which has its origins in simple nomadic recipes requiring few utensils. Gardener's Kebab is really a lamb and vegetable stew. The choice and amount of each vegetable is up to the cook.

1½ pounds boneless lamb
4 tablespoons butter
1 onion, chopped
2 large carrots, peeled and cut into sections
1 large can whole tomatoes (28 ounces)
2 to 3 cups chicken or beef stock
salt and pepper to taste

optional:

1 cup frozen green peas
1 small zucchini, sliced
½ pound string beans
1 green pepper, seeded and chopped
10 okra pods, cut up
2 cups eggplant, diced
1 large potato, peeled and cut into pieces
1 can chickpeas, drained

Trim all fat from the lamb. Cut the lamb into ¾ inch cubes.

In a large lidded saucepot, melt the butter and add the meat, onion, and carrots. Sauté until meat is lightly browned.

Add the tomatoes plus their liquid, the stock, salt, and pepper. Bring to a simmer, cover tightly, and cook for 45 minutes.

Other vegetables can be added at this time as desired. Choose at least three. Simmer another 30 minutes, or until the vegetables and meat are tender. Chickpeas should be added only during the last 10 minutes of cooking.

Watch liquid levels. Add more water or stock if needed. This is a stew, and it should be thick, without too much liquid when it is done.

Serve over Tomato Pilav or plain rice pilav. Serves 4 to 6.

Sis Kebab

The quintessential Turkish meal is sis kebab. Easy to prepare, its name means chunks of meat on a stick. The concept is very ancient, reaching back to the earliest nomadic tribes in Anatolia. Today, it can still be served with a flourish. Turkish skewers are of flattened metal, about eighteen inches long. Each one in a set is topped by a different brass ornament.

    1½ pounds boneless lamb
    2 tablespoons olive oil
    2 tablespoons lemon juice (½ lemon)
    1 medium onion, grated
    1 tablespoon fresh thyme, minced
      salt and pepper to taste
    8 cherry tomatoes
    1 green pepper, seeded and cut into 8 pieces
    8 large mushrooms, washed and dried
    8 pearl or green onions (long tops trimmed off)
      (4 skewers)

Trim fat from the meat, and cut into 1 inch cubes.

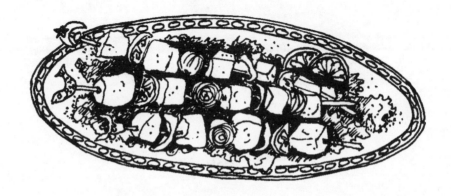

Mix together the oil, lemon juice, onion, thyme, salt, and pepper in a large bowl. Put the pieces in, toss to coat, cover, and refrigerate for 4 to 6 hours.

These are best cooked over a charcoal fire, but a hot broiler will do. Preheat.

Thread the meat pieces alternately with the vegetables onto the skewers.

Grill over medium heat, turning frequently. They are done when the vegetables are browned, and the meat is still pinkish inside.

Serve immediately with a pilav. Serves 4.

Iskender Kebabs

Named for the restaurateur who is said to have developed this recipe, the combination of ingredients that traditionally accompany these kebabs make them a favorite in Turkey. In restaurants the meat is the same as the grilled shaved meat used for doner kebabs. But that is impossible to reproduce at home, and so small grilled or fried kebabs are used.

1 pound boneless lamb
1 medium onion, grated
4 to 6 tablespoons olive oil (divided)
2 tablespoons lemon juice (½ lemon)
1 tablespoon fresh thyme, minced
   salt and pepper to taste
1 pint yogurt
2 cloves garlic, minced and divided
1 small onion, chopped
1 small can chopped tomatoes (14 ounces)
6 tablespoons butter
1 teaspoon paprika
⅛ teaspoon cayenne pepper
   (4 skewers)
4 large fresh pide (pita or pocket) breads

Trim all fat from the lamb and cut into ¾ inch cubes.

Mix grated onion, 2 tablespoons of the oil, lemon juice, thyme, salt, and pepper together in a bowl. Add the meat cubes, toss to coat, cover, and refrigerate for several hours.

Mix the yogurt with 1 clove of the minced garlic. Set aside.

To make the tomato sauce, heat 2 more tablespoons of the oil in a saucepan. Fry the other minced garlic clove, plus the small chopped onion.

Add the can of tomatoes and their liquid. Add salt and pepper to taste, and simmer gently for 30 minutes.

In another small pot, melt the butter and add the paprika and cayenne. Set aside.

Thread the meat kebabs equally onto the 4 skewers. Grill over a hot charcoal fire. This gives the best flavor, but they can also be done on an artificial charcoal fire or under a broiler. In a pinch, heat the last 2 tablespoons of oil in a large skillet and fry them. Any cooking method, though, must be quick, leaving the meat brown on the outside and slightly pink inside.

Place a warm pide bread on each of 4 plates. Spoon a bit of the hot melted butter mix onto each, then some tomato sauce, then some yogurt. Slide the cooked meat off each skewer onto the yogurt, and top with a bit more yogurt. Finally, drizzle the remaining butter mix equally on each serving, over the top of the final yogurt.

Serve immediately. Serves 4.

Lady's Thigh Kofte

Meatballs of all types are called kofte in Turkey. This delicious version can be served as tiny meze or, made larger, as a main dish. Their traditional shape is oval, hence the name. Dill, plus the Lemon and Egg Sauce which is served with them, are important flavors in this dish.

½ cup white rice
1 pound ground beef
1 large onion, grated
½ cup grated Parmesan cheese
¼ cup fresh parsley, minced
¼ cup fresh dill, minced
2 eggs, beaten
salt and pepper to taste
½ cup flour
½ cup vegetable oil for frying
Lemon and Egg Sauce, page 191

Simmer rice in 2 cups of water for 20 minutes. Drain thoroughly.

In a large mixing bowl, combine the rice, beef, onion, cheese, parsley, dill, eggs, salt, and pepper. Knead together with your hands for several minutes. The mix should be smooth and sticky.

Form meat mix into 1 inch ovals (for meze), or 3 inch ovals (for a main dish) with your hands. Roll each gently in the flour.

In a large skillet, heat the oil and fry the ovals on both sides until brown—about 8 minutes total. Do not crowd; do several batches if necessary.

Serve hot in Lemon and Egg Sauce. Serves 4 as a main dish.

Ground Beef and Eggs

This is a popular luncheon or simple supper dish in Turkey. Serve with Shepherd's Salad and lots of pide or French bread.

1 tablespoon butter
1 small onion, chopped
1 pound of ground beef
1 very ripe tomato, chopped
½ green pepper, diced
1 tablespoon fresh parsley, minced
  salt and pepper to taste
4 eggs

In a medium sized lidded skillet, melt the butter. Sauté the onion for several minutes, and add ground beef. Cook until the beef loses its pinkness, and becomes somewhat dry.

Add the tomato, pepper, parsley, salt, and pepper. Combine well, cover and simmer for 15 minutes.

Spread out the meat mix over the bottom of the pan, and create 4 hollows. Carefully break 1 egg into each depression, sprinkle with additional salt and pepper if desired, cover and cook on low until the eggs are set.

With a spatula, divide meat into 4 sections around the eggs, and lift onto four plates.

Serve immediately. Serves 4.

Circassian Chicken

This is the most well-known chicken dish in Turkey. It is often found on a raki table as a meze, or as the centerpiece of a more formal luncheon or dinner. It is always served cold.

    1 small chicken, or 2 pounds of chicken pieces
    1 carrot, cut in pieces
    1 onion, cut in half
    1 stalk celery, cut in half
    1 small bunch parsley
    1 teaspoon salt
      fresh ground pepper
      Tarator Sauce, page 193
    1 tablespoon butter
    1 teaspoon paprika
      walnut halves, parsley sprigs

The day before, place the chicken, carrot, onion, celery, parsley, salt, and pepper in a large saucepot. Cover with water, bring just to a boil, lower heat and simmer for 1 hour. Cool in its stock. Refrigerate.

The next day, strain off the stock and reserve ½ cup for use in the Tarator Sauce. Remove and discard the skin and bones from the chicken. Shred and tear the meat into bite-sized pieces. Mound the pieces in the center of a serving platter.

Completely mask the chicken mound with Tarator Sauce. Smooth the surface and clean off the edges of the platter.

Melt the butter in a small pot, and mix with the paprika to create a red oil. Drizzle over the top of the sauce. Press several walnut halves into the surface, and decorate with parsley sprigs.

Serve at room temperature. Serves 4 as part of a meal.

Herbed Chicken with Eggplant Purée

Everyone loves baked chicken breasts. The flavors of the herbs plus the Eggplant Purée used in this recipe blend to create a distinctively Turkish taste.

> 4 whole chicken breasts with skin
> 3 tablespoons olive oil
> 2 tablespoons fresh thyme, minced
> 1 tablespoon fresh rosemary, minced
> 1 teaspoon paprika
> ¼ teaspoon cayenne pepper
> 1 teaspoon salt
> Eggplant Purée, page 194

Split the 4 whole chicken breasts, to make 8 half breasts, leaving skin on. Wash and drain.

Mix the oil, thyme, rosemary, paprika, cayenne pepper, and salt in a deep bowl.

Coat each piece of chicken with the marinade. Lift the skin and work some of the herbs between it and the chicken.

Preheat the oven to 350°, and bake the chicken for about 45 minutes, or until golden.

Remove to a large serving dish and spoon Eggplant Purée alongside. Serve warm or hot. Serves 4 to 6.

Palace Chicken

This recipe is a cross between a chicken main dish and a pilav, and it was a question as to where to list it. The same recipe with less chicken, perhaps only one boned chicken breast cut into a small dice, would make a fine pilav side dish.

2 tablespoons olive oil
2 pounds cut up chicken pieces, with skin
2 tablespoons butter
1 large onion, diced
¼ cup pine nuts (pignolia)
2 cups white rice
1 small can chopped tomatoes (14 ounces)
¼ cup raisins
3½ cups chicken stock
½ cup fresh dill, chopped
   salt and pepper to taste

In a large deep skillet or saucepan with a tight fitting lid, heat the oil and brown the chicken pieces, turning until they are golden.

Lower the heat to simmer, add ¼ cup water, cover, and cook for 30 minutes. Check and add ¼ cup more water if they are still browning. After 30 minutes, remove the chicken pieces to a large platter.

In the same skillet, melt the butter and sauté the onion and nuts for 3 minutes. Add the rice, and stir to coat the grain with butter. Sauté for 1 minute. Add the tomatoes and their liquid, the raisins, chicken stock, dill, salt and pepper.

Bring just to a boil. Lower the heat to simmer, and stir well. Arrange the chicken pieces in the skillet on the rice mix. Add any drippings from the platter, cover the skillet and cook for 20 minutes.

Remove from the heat, uncover to release the steam, and cover with a towel for 10 minutes before serving.

Serve hot. Serves 6.

Roast Chicken with Pine Nut Stuffing

An ordinary roast chicken is elevated to a juicy feast with the addition of this very Turkish stuffing.

> 1 roasting chicken with innards
> 2 tablespoons butter
> 1 small onion, chopped
> ⅓ cup raisins
> ⅓ cup pine nuts (pignolia)
> 1 cup white rice
> 2 cups chicken stock
>   salt and pepper to taste

Take the bag of innards out of the chicken and find the liver in it. Discard the rest. Dice the liver. Rinse and drain the chicken.

In a lidded saucepan, melt the butter and sauté the liver and onion. After several minutes add the raisins and pine nuts. Sauté for 2 or 3 minutes more.

Add the rice and stir to coat with the butter. Pour in the chicken stock, bring to a boil, reduce heat to a simmer, cover the pot, and cook for 15 minutes. Remove from the heat, uncover, and allow to cool a bit.

Place the chicken in a roasting pan, breast side up. Stuff the cooked rice mix into the chicken until about two-thirds full. Sew up openings or use skewers.

Bake in a preheated 350° oven for about 1½ hours or until juices run clear from the breast or thighs. Baste every 20 minutes with drippings. Serves 4 to 6.

FISH AND SEAFOOD

THE VARIETY AND FRESHNESS of the seafood along the incredibly long coastline of Turkey is outstanding. In a country surrounded on three sides by water, only the towns of the interior are not well supplied. Istanbul is a true seafood lover's capital. There, it is possible to feast on dozens of varieties from the cold Black Sea, and the warmer Mediterranean.

The names may be different, but fish that resemble snapper, bass, mullet, pompano, bluefish, trout, bonito, and flounder abound. Swordfish steaks, shrimp, squid, and especially mussels are particular favorites of the Turkish people.

Finally, not to be forgotten is the famous Black Sea sturgeon and its caviar. Relatively inexpensive there, it is served with pride at the best raki tables.

The main cooking methods are grilling, frying, and baking. Most fish is served as a main course, but a few dishes are also served as meze.

Grilled Swordfish on Skewers

Along the coast, virtually all restaurants offer this simple dish. Typically, skewers of fish and meat are laid out on crushed ice, and the diner's choice is made directly, rather than from a menu. These are best if grilled over a real charcoal fire, just as they are done in Turkey.

1½ pounds swordfish steak
¼ teaspoon paprika
4 tablespoons lemon juice (1 lemon)
2 tablespoons olive oil
  salt and pepper to taste
  (4 skewers)
10 to 15 bay leaves
8 cherry tomatoes
1 green pepper, seeded and cut into 8 pieces
8 green onions, tops trimmed off
  Lemon Sauce, page 191

Trim off any skin and cut the swordfish into 1 inch cubes.

Mix the paprika, lemon, oil, salt, and pepper in a large bowl. Add fish cubes. Toss to coat, cover the bowl, and refrigerate for 4 to 5 hours.

Thread the fish cubes onto 4 skewers, evenly dividing and alternating them with the bay leaves and vegetables.

Grill over a hot charcoal fire for about 10 minutes, turning frequently.

Serve hot over pilav, accompanied by Lemon Sauce. Serves 4.

Baked Fish

The onions mixed with the fresh dill give a sweet flavor to this dish; the lemon and bay leaves are wonderfully aromatic.

1½ pounds boneless white fish fillets, such as cod
    salt and pepper to taste
  3 tablespoons butter
  4 large onions, sliced as thinly as possible
  ½ cup fresh dill, chopped
  2 lemons, sliced thin
20 bay leaves
    Lemon Sauce, page 191

Cut the fillets into portion-sized pieces if necessary. Sprinkle with salt and pepper, and set aside.

Heat the butter in a skillet. Sauté the onions very slowly over medium-low heat so that they cook without browning, about 15 minutes. Stir in the dill.

Transfer the onions and dill to a baking dish that will hold the fish fillets in a single layer. Spread out the onions to make a bed, and arrange the fish on top of them.

Cover the fish with lemon slices and bay leaves.

Bake in a preheated 350° oven for about 20 minutes or until the fish is firm and opaque.

Remove the bay leaves and discard all but 4 of them.

To serve, carefully lift the onions, fish, and lemon onto serving plates, and garnish each with one of the retained bay leaves.

Serve with Lemon Sauce. Serves 4.

Fish Patties

Serve these fish "kofte" cold as a meze or hot as a main dish.

1 pound white fish fillets or steak, such as cod
   or halibut
1 small onion, quartered
1 carrot, quartered
1 bay leaf
1 half lemon
   parsley sprigs
2 slices of good quality white bread, soaked in
   water
2 eggs, beaten
2 green onions, minced
¼ cup fresh dill, minced
¼ cup fresh parsley, minced
½ teaspoon allspice
   salt and pepper to taste
½ cup flour
1 cup vegetable oil for frying
   lemon wedges

Bring a pot of salted water to a boil. Drop in the onion, carrot, bay leaf, lemon (squeeze a bit into the water first), and parsley. Simmer for 15 minutes.

Put in the fish. Simmer gently for 10 minutes. Allow to cool out of the water. Then remove any skin and bones from the fish.

Squeeze water out of the bread, and place in a bowl with the fish, eggs, onions, dill, parsley, allspice, salt, and pepper. Knead with your hands until it is well mixed into a smooth paste.

Form into patties, either 1½ inches in diameter (for meze) or 3 inches in diameter (for a main dish). Gently coat with the flour.

Heat the vegetable oil in a skillet. Fry the patties without crowding, turning once, until golden. Drain on paper towels.

Serve hot or cold with lemon wedges. Serves 4 as a main dish.

Fish Plaki

"Plaki" refers to a way of cooking fish or vegetables that includes tomatoes, onions, garlic, and olive oil. Plaki is always served cold.

3 tablespoons olive oil
1 large carrot, peeled and sliced into ¼ inch rounds
1 stalk celery, chopped
1 large onion, chopped
2 cloves garlic, minced
1 large potato, peeled and cubed
　salt and pepper to taste
½ cup white wine
2 pounds firm white boneless fish fillets
2 very ripe tomatoes, sliced
1 lemon, sliced
¼ cup fresh parsley, chopped

In a large lidded skillet, heat the oil and sauté the carrot, celery, onion, garlic, and potato for 5 minutes.

Add salt, pepper, and white wine. Allow to bubble for a few minutes. Reduce the heat to a simmer and cover. Simmer for 15 minutes. Add ½ cup water if necessary.

Cut the fish into 2 inch pieces. Arrange the pieces over the simmered vegetables in a single layer. Arrange the tomato and lemon slices evenly over the top of the fish. Sprinkle with parsley, and additional salt and pepper. Cover and simmer for 5 minutes or until fish is cooked. Add a bit of water if necessary, but the finished dish should be rather dry.

Remove from the heat, uncover, and allow to cool. Carefully transfer to a serving plate and garnish with additional fresh lemon slices or wedges, and parsley if desired. Chill. Serves 4 to 6 as a main dish.

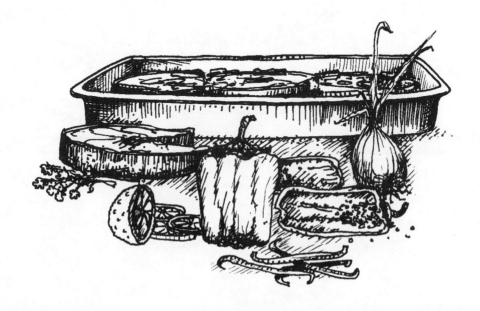

Salmon Casserole

Salmon, with its lovely color, looks especially appetizing when cooked with red and green peppers. Serve with a pilav.

        3 tablespoons olive oil
        1 clove garlic, minced
        1 large onion, thinly sliced
        2 large green peppers, seeded and sliced
        1 large red pepper, seeded and sliced
           salt and pepper to taste
        4 salmon steaks, 1 inch thick
        1 lemon, sliced
       ½ cup fresh parsley, chopped

In an oven proof casserole, heat the oil and slowly sauté the garlic, onion, green and red peppers for 7 minutes. Add salt, pepper, and ¼ cup water. Cover and simmer for a few minutes.

Remove most of the pepper mix from the casserole. Arrange the steaks on a thin bed of remaining pepper mix, and top with the rest.

Cover the peppers with the lemon slices, and sprinkle with the parsley.

Cover the casserole and bake in a preheated 350° oven for 30 minutes, or until fish is done.

Serve hot. Serves 4.

Raki Shrimp with Feta Cheese

This is definitely a party dish!

> 4 tablespoons olive oil (divided)
> 1 medium onion, chopped
> 1 clove garlic, minced
> 1 large can chopped tomatoes (28 ounces)
> 1 cup chicken stock
> ⅛ teaspoon cayenne pepper
>   salt to taste
> 2 pounds shelled raw shrimp
> ½ cup raki or other anise flavored liqueur (divided)
> ½ cup feta cheese, crumbled
>   lemon wedges, chopped parsley

In a saucepan, heat 2 tablespoons of oil, and sauté the onion and garlic. Add in the tomatoes plus their liquid, the stock and cayenne pepper. Salt to taste. Simmer and reduce uncovered for 30 minutes.

In a large skillet, heat the other 2 tablespoons of oil. Sauté the shrimp over high heat until they just turn pink. Pour in ¼ cup of the raki. Toss and sauté for another minute. Do not overcook.

Pour the reduced tomato mix over the shrimp. Stir, then pour all onto an oven proof serving platter. Sprinkle with the last ¼ cup of raki. Spread the feta cheese over all. Place under a hot broiler for several minutes until the cheese melts and browns a bit. Caution: especially with a gas flame broiler, the raki may ignite. If it does, pull the platter out, let it burn off the alcohol a moment, then blow it out, and return to the broiler if you wish. No harm done—it adds to the fun and drama!

Garnish with lemon wedges and parsley. Serve immediately with a pilav. Serves 6.

Stuffed Mussels

Stuffed mussels—"midya dolmasi" in Turkish, is an often served dish. Used either as a meze or as a main dish, they are festive and different.

    40 to 50 large mussels
    3 tablespoons olive oil
    3 large onions, chopped
    ¼ cup pine nuts (pignolia)
    ¼ cup raisins
    1 large ripe tomato, chopped
    ½ teaspoon allspice
    1 teaspoon sugar
    ½ teaspoon cinnamon
    ⅛ teaspoon nutmeg
    ⅛ teaspoon ground cloves
    salt and pepper to taste
    1 cup white rice
    2 cups chicken stock
    (clean white cotton string)
    1 lemon, cut in wedges
    parsley sprigs

Scrub the mussels, and remove any beard or bits of debris from the outside. Bring ½ inch of water to a boil in a large, deep lidded skillet, and place several mussels at a time in the skillet. Watch closely and remove them with a slotted spoon to a platter the instant they start to open. Continue until all the mussels are slightly open. Discard any that do not begin to open after 30 to 60 seconds in the boiling water. Save the water.

In a lidded saucepan, heat the oil and sauté the onions. Add the pine nuts, raisins, and tomato, and sauté for 3 more minutes. Add the allspice, sugar, cinnamon, nutmeg, cloves, salt, pepper, and rice. Stir to coat with oil.

Pour in the chicken stock, reduce heat to simmer, cover, and cook for 15 minutes. Remove from the heat, mix once, and allow to cool a bit.

Strain the water that cooked the mussels and set aside. Wipe out the skillet.

Open each mussel just enough to stuff in about 1 tablespoon of the rice mix. Do not separate the halves of the shell. Close the shell again, and firmly tie with a piece of string.

Wedge them tightly, hinge end down, into the skillet. Pour in 2 cups of the reserved water. Add plain water or stock if necessary to make 2 cups.

Cover the skillet, bring to a boil, then simmer for 30 minutes.

Allow mussels to cool uncovered in the skillet.

Refrigerate. At serving time, remove the strings or not, as you wish. Wipe each shell with a bit of oil to make them shine. Arrange on a serving platter with lemon wedges and parsley sprigs.

Serve chilled. Serves 6 as a main dish.

Mussel Pilav

Although technically a pilav (rice dish), if enough mussels are used, this is a delicious main course. Prepare in your best flameproof casserole so it can come right to the table.

    40 large mussels
     2 tablespoons olive oil
     1 large onion, chopped
    ¼ cup pine nuts (pignolia)
    ¼ cup raisins
     1 cup white rice
     1 small can chopped tomatoes (14 ounces)
     1 teaspoon sugar
     1 teaspoon cinnamon
    ½ teaspoon allspice
     2 cups canned beef stock
       salt and pepper to taste
    ½ cup fresh dill, chopped

Scrub mussels. Remove beard and any bits of surface debris. Set aside the 10 biggest.

Bring ½ inch of water to a boil in a saucepan. Drop the remaining 30 mussels in a few at a time and steam until they just open. Remove with a slotted spoon. Pry open the shells and remove the mussel. Discard the shells and any mussels that do not open. Set the mussels aside.

In the casserole, heat the oil and sauté the onion. Add the pine nuts, raisins, and rice. Sauté for 2 minutes. Pour in the tomatoes and their liquid, the sugar, cinnamon, allspice, beef stock, salt, and pepper. Lower the heat, stir, cover, and simmer for 10 minutes.

Uncover and gently stir in the 30 mussels. Cover and simmer for 5 more minutes.

Uncover and press the reserved 10 mussels, hinge side down, into the top of the rice. Cover and simmer for the last 10 minutes.

Uncover again. All 10 mussels should have opened on the top of the rice. Discard any that did not.

Drape a towel over the casserole and allow to rest for 20 minutes. Serve warm. Serves 4.

VEGETABLES

TURKISH COOKS TAKE a special pride in the preparation of vegetables. They are never simply boiled and served, but rather combined with other ingredients and most often lovingly slow-cooked in a minimum of fluid. Not a drop of flavor or nutrition is lost. A surprising number of vegetable dishes are served cold, even with a meal.

Of the four general categories of vegetable preparation, the first is "dolma" or stuffed. Zucchini, eggplant, peppers, and tomatoes are filled with rice or meat, and served either hot or cold. With meat these are considered main dishes.

Vegetables are also cooked "plaki" style—that is with onions, garlic, tomatoes, and olive oil—and served cold with separate meat and pilav.

Fried and fritter style vegetable dishes are common, and taste delicious with yogurt.

Lastly, there are substantial vegetable and meat stews.

Whichever way they are prepared, it is always with great care. The choice, variety, size, and quality of Turkey's vegetables is impressive, and over the centuries, cooks have discovered just how to bring out the best in them.

Be sure to check for delicious vegetable recipes in the meat (main dish), meze (appetizer), and salad sections of this book. Recipes are included in the section which indicates their most frequent "position" in a meal.

Spinach with Yogurt Sauce

A simple change makes creamed spinach very Turkish. Use full fat yogurt.

> 2 10-ounce packages frozen whole leaf spinach
> 2 tablespoons olive oil
> salt and pepper to taste
> 1 cup Yogurt Sauce, page 190
> paprika

Thaw spinach completely. Squeeze out all the water. It should be quite dry.

In a skillet, heat the oil and sauté the spinach for 10 minutes. Add salt and pepper to taste. Remove from the heat.

Lightly mix in the Yogurt Sauce and heat through if necessary. Transfer to a serving dish. Sprinkle with paprika. Serves 4 as a side dish.

Marinated Roast Peppers

Any variety of sweet green peppers can be used, but the long, light green Italian type are close to what is grown in Turkey. Serve cold as a side dish.

    6 bell peppers *or* 8 to 10 long sweet peppers
    2 cloves garlic, minced
    ¼ cup olive oil
    1 tablespoon vinegar
      salt and pepper to taste

Wash and dry the peppers. Roast them over a charcoal fire or under a broiler until the skin is charred and blistered.

Remove to a platter and cover with plastic wrap for 30 minutes. This will make it easier to peel the skin off them.

After they are skinned, remove the stem and seeds. Cut each into several large sections. Combine the garlic, oil, vinegar, salt and pepper in a bowl, and gently mix the peppers to coat. Allow them to marinate for several hours at room temperature. Serves 4 to 6 as a side dish.

Braised Leeks with Lemon and Egg Sauce

Leeks are a favorite fall vegetable, especially in eastern Turkey and northern Anatolia where it can become quite cold. Vegetables cooked in butter are always served hot in Turkey.

> 2 pounds leeks
> ¼ cup butter
> ¼ cup white rice
> 1 cup chicken stock
>   salt and pepper to taste
>   minced parsley
>   Lemon and Egg Sauce, page 191

Cut off and discard the root and most of the tough top leaves of the leeks. Wash well under running water to remove sand, and slice into 1 inch rounds.

Melt the butter in a large lidded skillet. Sauté the leeks for several minutes. Add the rice and stock. Mix together well.

Lower heat to a slow simmer, cover tightly and cook for 30 minutes.

Serve hot with warm Lemon and Egg Sauce. Serves 4 as a side dish.

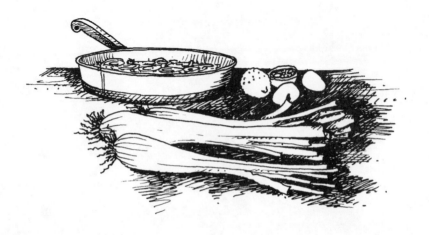

Braised Carrots Plaki

Plaki dishes, that is, food prepared with olive oil, onions, and tomatoes, are usually served at room temperature as a meze or side dish.

8 medium carrots
3 tablespoons olive oil
2 onions, sliced thin
1 large ripe tomato, diced
½ teaspoon sugar
½ cup chicken stock
  salt and pepper to taste
  fresh parsley, chopped
  lemon slices or wedges

Cut off stems and peel the carrots. Slice diagonally into ¼ inch ovals.

In a lidded saucepan, heat the oil and sauté the onions for 5 minutes.

Add the carrots, tomato, sugar, stock, salt, and pepper. Lower heat to simmer and braise about 45 minutes, or until carrots are tender. Check the liquid level as they cook and add water if necessary. There should be almost none left at the end.

Cool in the pot. Transfer to a serving platter, and garnish with parsley and lemon. Serves 4 to 6 as a side dish.

Zucchini with Fresh Herbs

In mid-summer, when zucchini are growing faster than they can be harvested and prepared, cooks are on the lookout for yet another way to serve them!

    3 medium zucchini
    3 tablespoons olive oil
    2 medium onions, chopped
    6 cloves garlic, minced
    1 large, ripe tomato, diced
    ¼ cup fresh dill, chopped
    ¼ cup fresh mint, chopped
    ½ cup fresh parsley, chopped
    ½ teaspoon sugar
      salt and pepper to taste
    ¼ cup water

Wash and dry the zucchini. Remove the stems and slice zucchini into ¼ inch round slices.

In a deep, lidded saucepan, heat the oil and sauté the onions and garlic for 3 minutes.

Add the zucchini. Sauté for 5 minutes.

Add the tomato, dill, mint, parsley, sugar, salt, and pepper. Sauté for 3 minutes.

Add water, reduce heat to a simmer and cook for no longer than 5 minutes. Do not overcook.

Serve hot or cold. Serves 4 as a side dish.

Zucchini Boats with Cheese

Choose small to medium zucchini for this dish, so that they are not too watery.

                4 or 5 zucchini, depending on size
                ¾ cup Swiss type cheese, grated
                ½ cup feta cheese, crumbled
                2 eggs, beaten
                ¼ cup fresh parsley, minced
                ¼ cup fresh dill, minced
                1 tablespoon flour
                   salt and pepper to taste
                3 tablespoons butter

Wash and dry zucchini. Cut off stems. Slice in half lengthwise. With a melon scoop or spoon, scoop out the seeds along each length.

Bring a large pot of salted water to a boil. Drop in the zucchini and cook for 10 to 12 minutes or until tender but not limp.

Arrange the zucchini, cut sides up, side by side in a greased oven pan.

In a bowl, mix together the two cheeses, eggs, parsley, dill, flour, salt, and pepper.

Fill each zucchini boat with some of the cheese mix. Dot with butter. Broil under a preheated broiler until the cheese is brown and bubbly. Serves 6 to 8 as a side dish.

Savory Artichokes

Using the canned artichoke pieces makes this a quick, easy vegetable side dish.

> 2 tablespoons olive oil
> 1 onion, diced
> 2 cloves garlic, minced
> ¾ cup frozen mixed carrots and peas
> 3 14-ounce cans of artichoke bottoms or hearts (not marinated)
> ½ teaspoon sugar
> salt and pepper to taste
> 4 tablespoons lemon juice (1 lemon)
> fresh dill, chopped

In a lidded skillet, heat the oil and sauté the onion and garlic for 5 minutes.

Add the carrots, peas, drained artichokes, sugar, salt, and pepper.

Add water to the lemon juice to make ½ cup total. Pour into the skillet. Lower heat, cover and braise for 20 minutes.

Allow to cool. Transfer to a serving platter and garnish with dill. Serve at room temperature. Serves 6 as a side dish.

Stuffed Artichokes with Dill

Artichokes, stuffed and baked like this, make an attractive first course or vegetable side dish. Cook artichokes a long time and then allow them to gain flavor by refrigerating overnight.

4 large artichokes
3 tablespoons olive oil (divided)
1 medium onion, diced
½ cup rice
1 cup chicken stock
  salt and pepper to taste
½ cup fresh dill, chopped
4 lemon slices
  Lemon and Egg Sauce, page 191

Wash the artichokes. Cut off the stems so they will stand. Slice off about ½ inch of the top. With a scissors, trim the end off each leaf.

Stand the artichokes in ½ inch of water in a deep lidded saucepot. Sprinkle salt over them. Bring the water to a boil, lower to a simmer, and cook for 30 minutes. Remove from the water and allow to cool.

Then gently open the artichokes without breaking them, and scoop out the fuzzy choke with a spoon.

In a lidded saucepot, heat 1 tablespoon of the oil and sauté the onion. Add the rice, stock, salt, and pepper to taste. Bring to a boil, reduce to a simmer, and cook for 15 minutes.

Uncover and stir in the dill. Cover and cook for 5 more minutes. Cool.

Grease an oven proof casserole big enough to hold the four artichokes upright. Open the artichokes enough to spoon and press ¼ of the rice mix into each. Place them in the casserole and top each with a lemon slice. Drizzle remaining 2 tablespoons of oil over the top of all.

Pour ½ cup of boiling water around the artichokes, cover, and bake in a preheated 350° oven for 40 minutes.

Allow to cool, serve at room temperature with warm Lemon and Egg Sauce on the side for dipping.

Basic Rice (Vegetarian) Stuffing for Vegetables

This recipe will fill about 20 assorted vegetables.

¼ cup olive oil
2 medium onions, diced
½ cup pine nuts (pignolia)
½ cup raisins
1 small can chopped tomatoes (14 ounces)
1 teaspoon sugar
¼ cup fresh mint, chopped
¼ cup fresh dill, chopped
½ cup fresh parsley, chopped
½ teaspoon cinnamon
½ teaspoon allspice
salt and pepper to taste
2 cups white rice
3 cups chicken stock or water

In a large lidded saucepot, heat the oil and sauté the onions, pine nuts, and raisins.

Add the tomatoes and their liquid, sugar, mint, dill, parsley, cinnamon, allspice, salt, pepper, rice, and stock.

Bring to a boil, reduce to a simmer, cover and cook for 20 minutes.

Uncover, mix once and allow to cool. Proceed as directed.

Basic Meat (and Rice) Stuffing for Vegetables

This recipe will fill 15 to 20 assorted vegetables.

        2 tablespoons olive oil
    1½ pounds ground lamb or beef
        1 large onion, diced
        1 small can chopped tomatoes (14 ounces)
      ¼ cup fresh mint, chopped
      ¼ cup fresh dill, chopped
      ½ cup parsley, chopped
          salt and pepper to taste
    1½ cups white rice
    2½ cups beef stock

In a large lidded saucepot, heat the oil and sauté the meat and onion. Add the tomatoes and their liquid, mint, dill, parsley, salt, pepper, rice, and stock.

Bring to a boil, reduce to a simmer, cover and cook for 15 minutes.

Uncover, mix once and allow to cool. Proceed as directed.

Vegetable Dolmas

Stuffed vegetable dishes (dolmas) such as these are the pride of Turkish cooks. Some restaurants specialize in them. Either of the preceding stuffing mixtures can be used with tomatoes, eggplant, green bell peppers, or zucchini. Try a mixture of all of the possibilities. They are quite filling and with bread and a salad, make a fine meal.

To prepare:

Eggplant—Choose the smallest eggplants, long and narrow. Wash and dry. Remove the stems and peel off a 1 inch wide strip of skin from top to bottom. In the peeled area, make a long deep cut in the eggplant, but don't pierce the bottom. Scoop out and discard some of the inside on either side of the cut and gently spread the eggplant open to make a hollowed out boat shape. Fill with either rice mix, page 156 or page 157.

Peppers—Choose large uniform bell peppers. Wash and dry. Cut a circle around the top. Remove and save the tops. Scoop out the seeds and membrane. Fill with either rice mix, page 156 or page 157. Replace the tops.

Zucchini—Choose medium sized zucchini. Wash and dry. Cut off the stems and cut each zucchini into three barrel-shaped sections. Carefully scoop out most of the seeds and pulp, being careful to not cut through the bottom. They should look like cylindrical cups. Fill with either rice mix, page 156 or page 157.

Tomatoes—Choose firm, ripe tomatoes of uniform size. Wash and dry. Make a circular cut in the top and save it. Scoop out and discard the seeds, pulp, and juice to leave a cup shape. Fill with either rice mix, page 156 or page 157. Replace the tops on the tomatoes.

To cook:

> parsley or dill stems
> ¼ pound of butter
> tomato slices
> 1½ cups tomato juice

Line a heavy roasting pan or casserole with parsley or dill stems. Place the stuffed vegetables tightly side by side; tomato, pepper, and zucchini pieces upright, and eggplant boats on their side.

Dot the top of each vegetable with butter. Place tomato slices on the eggplant.

Carefully pour 1 to 1½ cups of tomato juice around the vegetables.

Cover with cooking parchment and tuck in the edges. Tightly cover the roasting pan or casserole with a lid or heavy foil. Bake in a preheated 350° oven for 45 minutes, or until the vegetables are tender. Add a little water if necessary halfway through. Allow to cool in the baking pan.

Serve warm or at room temperature.

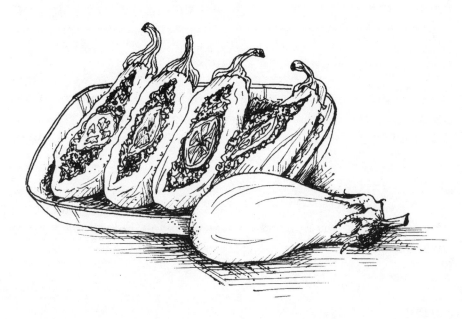

Eggplant Kebab

The popular eggplant has dozens of traditional preparations in Turkey. In this vegetable main dish the meat may be used ground or cubed.

>   2 medium eggplants
>   4 tablespoons olive oil (divided)
>   1½ pounds lean lamb, ground or cut into ½ inch
>   cubes
>   2 medium onions, chopped
>   2 large ripe tomatoes
>   salt and pepper to taste
>   ½ cup parsley, chopped

Wash and dry eggplants. Remove stems and peel the eggplant lengthwise to create ½ inch stripes.

Slice in 1 inch thick rounds. Salt each side generously, and let stand for 30 minutes. Rinse the slices and pat very dry with paper towels.

Heat 1 tablespoon of oil in a large skillet. Brown one side of the eggplant slices and remove from the pan. Heat another tablespoon of oil. Return slices to the pan and brown the other side. Line the bottom of a large greased baking pan with the slices.

Heat the remaining 2 tablespoons of oil in the skillet, and sauté the meat and onion for 8 minutes. Dice one tomato and add it, plus salt, pepper, and parsley to the skillet with the meat. Sauté for 5 minutes.

Spread the cooked meat mix over the eggplant slices.

Slice the second tomato, and place slices of it over the meat.

Pour one cup of water over all, cover tightly and bake for 1 hour in a preheated 350° oven.

Serve hot with a pilav. Serves 4.

Eggplant Imam Bayildi

Imam Bayildi is the most famous vegetable dish originating in Turkey. Its name means "the priest fainted," and it is just one of the dozens of ways to prepare eggplant. Whether or not the holy man fainted from the love of the dish, or upon learning how much olive oil was used in its preparation, is uncertain.

    6 to 8 small long eggplants
    ½ cup olive oil
    3 onions, sliced thin
    7 cloves garlic, minced
    2 green peppers, diced
    ½ cup fresh parsley, minced
    2 ripe tomatoes, chopped
    ¼ teaspoon cayenne pepper
        salt to taste
    1 cup chicken stock
        extra tomato slices
        lemon slices

Wash and dry the eggplants. Cut almost in half lengthwise, being careful to not cut all the way through.

Heat half of the oil in a skillet and fry the eggplants until the skin is brown, about 3 minutes. Remove and set aside.

Add the rest of the oil to the skillet, and sauté the onions, garlic, and peppers. After 5 minutes, add the parsley, tomatoes, pepper and salt. Sauté another 5 minutes.

Grease a large baking pan. Open the eggplants somewhat flat, and stuff them with the sautéed vegetable mix. Wedge them into the pan, closing them a little. Top with tomato and lemon slices and drizzle any oil left in the pan over the top.

Pour the stock into the pan around the eggplants, cover, and bake in a preheated 350° oven for 1 hour. Cool in the pan. Serve at room temperature. Serves 6 to 8.

Cabbage and Beef Casserole

This is a delicious cold weather stew. Serve with a pilav, tomato salad, and lots of fresh bread.

  ¼ pound butter
  1½ pounds lean boneless beef, cut in ¾ inch cubes
  2 medium onions, chopped
  1 small can chopped tomatoes (14 ounces)
  1 medium head of cabbage
  ¼ teaspoon cayenne pepper
  1 teaspoon sugar
  salt to taste

In a large, lidded saucepot, heat the butter. Slowly brown the beef and onions, about 10 minutes.

Add tomatoes and their liquid. Cut the cabbage into 8 wedges. Add to the pot along with the pepper, sugar, and salt.

Mix well, lower the heat to simmer, cover and cook for 1 to 1½ hours, or until meat is tender. Add boiling water if necessary from time to time, but most liquid should be absorbed when the meat is done.

Serve hot. Serves 4.

Mixed Greens and Beef Kebab

Kebabs (cubed meat or fish) can be slow cooked with vegetables, as well as grilled.

4 tablespoons butter
1½ pounds lean boneless beef, cut into ¾ inch cubes
3 onions, chopped
1 clove garlic, minced
1½ pounds of fresh mixed greens: chard, escarole, or spinach
2 medium potatoes, peeled and cut into 1 inch cubes
1 teaspoon sugar
1 cup beef stock
salt and pepper to taste

In a large lidded saucepot, melt the butter. Slowly brown the beef, onions and garlic for 8 minutes. Pour in ½ cup water, lower the heat and braise for 30 minutes.

Wash the greens. Add them to the meat, along with the potato, sugar, salt, pepper, and stock. Bring to a boil and mix well to wilt the greens. Lower the heat, cover and cook for 45 minutes.

Serve hot with fresh bread and a tomato salad. Serves 4.

Cabbage Meat Dolmas

Recipes similar to this are found in most of the cuisines of eastern Europe. The Lemon and Egg Sauce makes ours particularly Turkish.

> 1 medium cabbage
> 1 pound lean ground lamb
> ⅓ cup white rice
> 1 small can chopped tomatoes (14 ounces)
> ¼ cup fresh dill, chopped
> ½ cup fresh parsley, chopped
>   salt and pepper to taste
> 4 tablespoons butter
>   Lemon and Egg Sauce, page 191

Bring a large pot of salted water to a boil. Core the cabbage deeply, and lower it into the water. After a few minutes remove the outer leaves with tongs and set aside. Continue to boil, and every 3 to 4 minutes carefully remove the next layer of leaves. When you get to the inner cabbage where the leaves are too small, stop. Reserve the inside and torn leaves.

Knead together the lamb, uncooked rice, tomatoes and their juice, dill, parsley, salt and pepper in a bowl.

Line the bottom of a roasting pan with the reserved small and torn leaves. Trim the hard vein out of the whole leaves.

One at a time, lay out a leaf and put 2 tablespoons of the meat mix in the center. Fold in the sides and roll, starting from the thick end. Place the cabbage rolls tightly side by side, seam side down, in the roasting pan.

When all rolls are completed, pour 1½ cups of water over them, dot with butter and wrap pan tightly with foil.

Bake in a preheated 350° oven for 1 hour. Allow to cool a bit. Remove to a serving platter. Pour half of the Lemon and Egg Sauce over the rolls, and pass the other half in a small dish to guests. Serves 4 as a main dish.

White Beans and Lamb Stew

In Turkey, lamb and bean stews are a great favorite, especially in winter. Lentils, kidney beans or chickpeas are commonly used, but the most traditional is made with white beans and is called Janissary Stew. The Janissaries were the sultan's own soldiers.

4 tablespoons butter
1½ pounds of boneless lean lamb, cut into ¾ inch cubes
2 medium onions, chopped
1 large can chopped tomatoes (28 ounces)
3 cups of beef stock
¼ teaspoon cayenne pepper or more
salt to taste
2 15-ounce cans of Great Northern beans, drained

In a large lidded saucepot, melt the butter and slowly sauté the meat and onion until brown.

Add the tomatoes, stock, pepper, and salt. Lower heat to a simmer, cover and cook for 1 hour.

Add the beans, mix well and simmer for 15 minutes.

Serve hot with a pilav, green salad and bread. Serves 4.

SALADS

VEGETABLES, SO PLENTIFUL and fresh throughout Turkey, are used in cold, light salads as part of virtually every meal.

In addition to the mixed greens and raw vegetable salads, simply dressed with oil and lemon, Turkish cooks show off with a variety of cooked vegetable salads.

Cooked or raw, salads are often served with yogurt, feta cheese, olives and bread to make a complete light lunch.

Tomato and Cucumber Salad

It couldn't be simpler, but only make this salad when the best summer-time tomatoes are available.

> 2 large, fully ripe summer tomatoes
> 1 cucumber, peeled and thinly sliced
> 1 small onion, thinly sliced
> Lemon Sauce, page 191

Cut the tomatoes in 8 sections each. Combine with the cucumber and onion.

Mix with Lemon Sauce.

Refrigerate for 30 minutes before serving. Serves 4.

Mixed Greens Salad

Mixed green salads such as this are served with fried or grilled meats and fish. In the countryside, dandelion and cress, plus fresh herbs such as dill and chives are added.

> Enough Romaine, Boston, spinach, arugula, etc.,
> leaves to make salad for 6
> Lemon Sauce, page 191

optional:

> calamata olives
> crumbled feta cheese
> crumbled hard boiled egg

Wash and dry leaves. Tear into bite sized pieces.

Pour Lemon Sauce over leaves in a large salad bowl. Toss well. Serve immediately with optional garnishes. Serves 6.

Shepherd's Salad

This is the most common salad in Turkey, served in all restaurants and homes. It is especially good with broiled or fried meat and fish dishes.

enough Boston and Romaine lettuce for 6 servings
2 fully red ripe tomatoes, cut into 6 wedges each
½ cucumber, peeled, seeded and thinly sliced
½ green bell pepper, seeded and sliced
4 or 5 pepperoncini peppers, sliced into rings
½ small onion, thinly sliced
3 radishes, thinly sliced
12 black calamata olives
1 tablespoon fresh dill, minced
1 tablespoon fresh mint, minced
1 tablespoon vinegar
Lemon Sauce, page 191

Wash and dry the lettuce. Break into pieces. Place leaves plus all other ingredients in a large salad bowl. Add the Lemon Sauce. Toss. Serve immediately. Serves 6.

Cucumber Yogurt Salad

Called cacik in Turkey, this popular, cool and refreshing salad uses the same ingredients as the soup, also called cacik (see: Cold Cucumber and Yogurt Soup, page 96). It merely changes proportions.

2 large cucumbers
1 cup yogurt
1 clove garlic, minced
1 teaspoon olive oil
1 teaspoon vinegar
¼ cup fresh mint, chopped
salt and pepper to taste

Peel the cucumbers and slice thinly.

Combine the yogurt, garlic, oil, vinegar, mint, salt, and pepper. Pour over the cucumbers.

Mix together well, cover and refrigerate for several hours.

Serve well chilled. Serves 4 to 6.

Bean Salad

Lots of beans are consumed in Turkey, mainly in stews, vegetable preparations, and salads. Any kind can be used in this salad, but it is usually made with white beans.

2 15-ounce cans of Great Northern beans, drained
½ green bell pepper, diced
1 ripe tomato, diced
½ small onion, thinly sliced
¼ cup fresh dill, chopped
1 tablespoon vinegar
Lemon Sauce, page 191

In a deep bowl, combine the beans, pepper, tomato, onion, dill, vinegar, and Lemon Sauce. Mix well, cover and refrigerate overnight. Serves 6.

Cold Zucchini Salad

Try this unusual salad with a rich stew.

> 4 medium zucchini
> ½ cup yogurt
> ¼ cup fresh dill, chopped
> 1 clove garlic, minced
> 1 teaspoon vinegar
> 1 teaspoon olive oil
>   salt and pepper to taste
> 1 ripe tomato, diced

Wash the zucchini. Remove stems. Slice into ¼ inch rounds.

Bring a large pot of salted water to a boil. Boil the zucchini for 10 minutes or until tender but not too soft. Drain. Refresh in cold water. Drain again.

In a small bowl, mix the yogurt, dill, garlic, vinegar, oil, salt, and pepper.

Pour over the zucchini, toss to coat, cover and refrigerate for several hours.

Transfer to a serving platter and scatter the diced tomatoes over the top. Serves 6.

Beet and Yogurt Salad

This is a different and pretty salad to serve.

>   4 to 5 beets
> ½ cup yogurt
>   1 clove garlic, minced
>   2 tablespoons lemon juice (½ lemon)
>   2 tablespoons olive oil
>   salt and pepper to taste
>   1 green onion, chopped

Boil the beets in salted water for 1 hour or until easily pierced with a fork. Remove from the water and, when cool enough to handle, slip the skins off. Slice thinly and place in a deep bowl.

In a separate bowl, combine yogurt, garlic, lemon juice, oil, salt, pepper, and onion. With a wire whisk, mix everything together well.

Pour dressing over the beets, and gently mix. Refrigerate until thoroughly chilled, or overnight.

At serving time, gently mix again. Transfer to a serving dish. Serves 4 to 6.

Cauliflower Tarator

This is a traditional cauliflower preparation in Turkey, but will seem new to our palettes. It is a surprisingly delicious salad.

> 1 tablespoon salt
> 1 medium cauliflower
> 4 tablespoons lemon juice (1 lemon)
> Tarator Sauce, page 193

Bring a large pot of water to a boil. Put in the salt, cauliflower, and lemon juice. Boil for 15 to 20 minutes or until tender. Do not over-cook.

Drain, let cool, and separate the flowerets. Arrange on a serving platter.

Pour Tarator Sauce over the cool cauliflower. Refrigerate.

Serve at room temperature. Serves 6.

Eggplant Salad

This excellent eggplant salad has an unexpected taste.

    1 large eggplant
  ¼ cup olive oil
    1 large sweet red pepper
    1 small hot chili pepper, seeded and minced
    2 tablespoons lemon juice (½ lemon)
  ½ cup yogurt
    1 tablespoon olive oil
    2 cloves garlic, minced
      salt to taste
    1 ripe tomato, cubed
    6 to 12 calamata olives

Wash and dry the eggplant. Cut into ¾ inch cubes. Generously salt the cubes and allow to rest for 30 minutes. Rinse off the salt and pat the eggplant quite dry on paper towels.

Heat the ¼ cup of olive oil in a large skillet until very hot. Sauté the eggplant cubes until browned. Remove from the skillet and drain on paper towels.

Roast the red pepper under a broiler until its skin is blistered. Immediately place in a plastic bag or close in foil for 15 minutes. Then pull the skin off the pepper and remove the seeds. Cut into narrow strips.

Place the drained eggplant, the red pepper strips, and the hot chili pepper into a salad bowl.

Put the lemon juice, yogurt, 1 tablespoon of olive oil, garlic, and salt into a food processor. Whirl for a few seconds to combine. Or, mix together in a bowl.

Pour the dressing over the eggplant and peppers. Toss well to coat. Refrigerate for a few hours. At serving time, toss again with the tomato. Transfer to serving plates. Garnish with olives. Serves 6.

PILAVS

RICE IS PRESENT IN SOME FORM in most Turkish main meals. It is the staple grain of middle class and urban people, although poorer country folk use bulgur (cracked wheat) in its place.

Really native to the regions east of Turkey, it gained popularity during the Seljuk and Ottoman periods. Its correct and painstaking preparation at Topkapi Palace was the mark of their greatest chefs.

In a traditional Turkish meal from that era, pilav was presented as a separate course just before dessert, but today is served with the main dishes.

Pilav refers to the preparation of rice or bulgur in stock, with or without other ingredients. Ideally, careful proportioning of grain and liquid results in the complete absorption of stock at the exact moment the grain is finished. The use of basmati or long grain white rice is most typical.

The combining of stock and rice plus vegetables, nuts, fruit, shellfish, meat, and herbs to create the savory dishes known as pilavs is completely Turkish.

Grape Pilav

Plain rice pilavs are sometimes combined with fruits, such as dried or fresh apricots. White seedless grapes are also a popular choice.

2 tablespoons butter
1½ cups white rice, rinsed well and drained
2¾ cups chicken stock
salt and pepper to taste
2 cups seedless white grapes, off the stems

In a lidded saucepot, melt the butter and sauté the rice for 1 minute.

Pour in the stock, salt, and pepper. Bring to a boil, lower the heat to a simmer and cook for 17 minutes.

Uncover, gently fold in the grapes, being careful not to break the grapes or the rice.

Cover with a towel and let rest for 10 minutes.

Serves 4 to 6.

Tomato Pilav

Tomato pilav is good served alone, or it can be used as a vegetable stuffing.

> 4 tablespoons butter
> 1 small onion, diced
> 1 clove garlic, minced
> 1 small can chopped tomatoes (14 ounces)
> ¼ cup fresh parsley, chopped
> ¼ cup fresh basil or dill, chopped
> 1½ cups white rice, rinsed well and drained
> 2½ cups beef stock
>   pinch of cayenne pepper
>   salt to taste

In a lidded saucepot, heat the butter and sauté the onion and garlic for 3 minutes.

Pour in the tomatoes and their liquid, parsley, and basil or dill.

Add the rice, stock, cayenne pepper, and salt. Bring to a boil, reduce heat to a simmer, cover and cook for 17 minutes.

Remove from the heat, uncover to release the steam. Let rest for 10 minutes covered by a towel.

Serves 4 to 6.

Pilav with Chickpeas

The ingredients of this pilav are particularly nutritious.

4 tablespoons butter
1 small onion, diced
1 clove garlic, minced
1 small can chopped tomatoes, drained (14 ounces)
1½ cups white rice, rinsed well and drained
2¾ cups canned chicken stock
salt and pepper to taste
1 15-ounce can chickpeas, drained

In a lidded saucepot, heat the butter and sauté the onions and garlic for 3 minutes.

Add the drained tomatoes, and sauté another 3 minutes.

Add the rice, stock, salt and pepper. Bring to a boil, then lower the heat, cover, and simmer for 7 minutes.

Uncover and stir in the chickpeas. Cover and simmer for 10 more minutes. Remove from the heat and uncover to release the steam. Let rest for 10 minutes covered by a towel.

Serves 4 to 6.

Minted Pea Pilav

This pilav is especially nice with grilled lamb chops.

3 tablespoons butter
1 small onion, chopped
1½ cup white rice, well rinsed and drained
2¾ cups chicken stock
¼ cup fresh mint, chopped
1 cup frozen peas
salt and pepper to taste

In a lidded saucepot, heat the butter and sauté the onion for 3 minutes.

Add the rice, and stir to coat with the butter for 1 minute.

Add the stock, mint, peas, salt, and pepper. Bring to a boil, reduce to a simmer, cover and cook for 17 minutes.

Uncover to release the steam. Let rest for 10 minutes covered by a towel.

Serves 4 to 6.

Bulgur Pilav

Bulgur (cracked wheat) can be purchased in most supermarkets and in shops specializing in Middle Eastern foods. It is used more frequently in the countryside of Turkey and is heartier than rice pilav. It is a good complement to stews and roasts.

    3 tablespoons butter
    1 medium onion, chopped
    1 cup bulgur
    2 cups beef stock
       salt and pepper to taste

In a lidded saucepot, melt the butter and sauté the onion for 5 minutes.

Stir in the bulgur. Sauté for 2 more minutes.

Pour in the stock. Add the salt and pepper. Bring to a boil, then lower the heat to simmer, cover, and cook for 20 to 25 minutes. The bulgur should be tender but firm, and not mushy.

Serves 4.

Chicken Liver Pilav

This particular combination of ingredients, called ic pilav, is very popular. It forms the base of many stuffings for vegetables and fowl, as well as being excellent on its own with roasts.

4 tablespoons butter
¼ pound chicken livers, diced
1 small onion, diced
¼ cup pine nuts (pignolia)
¼ cup raisins
1½ cups white rice, rinsed well and drained
2¾ cups chicken stock
salt and pepper to taste

In a lidded saucepot, heat the butter and sauté the liver, onion, and pine nuts for 5 minutes.

Add the raisins and rice. Mix and sauté for 3 more minutes.

Pour in the stock. Add salt and pepper. Bring to a boil. Lower the heat to a simmer, cover and cook for 17 minutes.

Remove from the heat and uncover to release the steam. Let rest for 10 minutes covered by a towel.

Serves 4 to 6.

SAUCES

THERE ARE VERY FEW SAUCES in the Turkish cuisine. Most recipes create their own through slow cooking, and additional enhancement is not deemed necessary. But the six principal ones that follow are quick and easy. They are used on salads, soups, meats, and vegetables, and are indispensable in a few classic recipes such as Circassian Chicken and Sultan's Delight.

Yogurt Sauce

Turkish people dearly love yogurt, so it is no accident that one of their most popular sauces is made with it. Serve with cold vegetables, vegetable fritters, and meat.

> 1 cup yogurt
> 1 clove garlic, minced or crushed
> ½ teaspoon salt

Combine yogurt, garlic, and salt. Cover and chill for several hours. Use as directed.

Tomato Sauce

This sauce is used over eggplant and other vegetables, either hot or cold.

> 2 tablespoons olive oil
> 1 clove garlic, minced
> 1 small onion, diced
> 1 small can chopped tomatoes (14 ounces)
> ¼ cup fresh parsley, minced
> 1 bay leaf
> 1 tablespoon fresh basil, minced
> salt and pepper to taste

Heat the oil and sauté the garlic and onion for 3 minutes.

Add the tomatoes and their liquid, parsley, bay leaf, basil, salt, and pepper.

Simmer for 15 minutes. Remove the bay leaf. Use as directed.

Lemon Sauce

Lemon Sauce is used mainly as a salad and fish dressing.

2 tablespoons olive oil
4 tablespoons lemon juice (1 lemon)
¼ cup fresh parsley, minced
salt and pepper to taste

Whisk all ingredients together. Use as directed.

Lemon and Egg Sauce

This sauce is one of the most common in Turkey, and is used in soups, and over meatballs and vegetables.

2 eggs
4 tablespoons lemon juice (1 lemon)
½ cup water or chicken stock
salt and pepper to taste

Beat eggs well. Pour into a small saucepan with the lemon juice, water or stock, salt, and pepper.

Slowly raise the heat, and whisk constantly until the sauce thickens. Do not allow to boil.

Use as directed.

Tarator Sauce

Tarator Sauce is used on Circassian Chicken, with mussels, over boiled cauliflower, and with other boiled vegetables. A blender or food processor makes its preparation quick and easy.

1 cup chopped walnuts
4 slices of good quality white bread, broken up
2 cloves garlic, sliced
2 tablespoons lemon juice (½ lemon)
½ cup chicken stock
  salt and pepper to taste
¾ cup olive oil

Place the walnuts, bread, garlic, lemon juice, chicken stock, salt and pepper in a food processor. Whirl for a few seconds until smooth.

Slowly add the oil in a stream through the container top opening, while running the processor. The result should look like a mayonnaise. Use as directed.

Eggplant Purée

Used mainly with Sultan's Delight, but is sometimes served alone as a side dish.

> 1 large eggplant
> 3 tablespoons butter
> 2 tablespoons flour
> ¾ cup milk
>   salt and pepper to taste
> ⅔ cup grated Parmesan, Romano, and Swiss-type
>   cheese (total)

Roast the eggplant over a charcoal fire, in the flames on a gas stove top, or under a broiler. When the flesh is soft and the skin is charred allow to cool.

Cut open the eggplant and scoop out the insides. Squeeze out all of the water. Transfer to a food processor and purée.

In a saucepan, melt the butter. With a wire whisk, mix in the flour. Cook gently for a minute, then add the milk. Whisk vigorously. Raise the heat and stir until the mix is thick. Simmer for 5 minutes, stirring constantly. Add salt and pepper.

Add in the cheeses and the eggplant. Stir and cook for 5 minutes until all is hot and bubbly. Serve immediately.

BREAD

BREAD IS SERVED WITH EVERY MEAL in Turkey, great stacks of it in restaurants. It is fresh, chewy, and addictively good. It comes in fat loaves, and resembles the best Italian-style white breads.

A variation in shape is the flat pide (pita or pocket) bread, which is used under or around doner kebabs. Pide can be purchased in most supermarkets here.

We have included a recipe for simit, the donut-shaped sesame seed bread, which is sold on the street as a snack.

Simit

Simit is stacked on long sticks, and sold by street vendors all over Turkey.

> 2 packages active dry yeast
> 1½ cups barely warm water
> 1½ cups barely warm milk
> 2 tablespoons sugar
> 2 teaspoons salt
> 2 tablespoons vegetable oil
> 6 to 8 cups flour
> 1 egg
> ¾ cup sesame seeds

Dissolve yeast in the warm water in a large bowl. Stir in the milk, sugar, salt, oil, and 3 cups of the flour. Whisk well for 2 minutes.

Add one cup additional flour at a time, stirring with a big spoon, until it becomes too difficult to add more.

You should have a stiff dough that does not stick to your hands. Start to knead it, and add more flour at this time if it's too sticky.

Knead on a floured surface for 4 minutes or until the dough is smooth and elastic.

Place the dough in a greased bowl, and grease the top surface of the dough. Cover with plastic wrap and keep in a warm place for 45 minutes.

Dough should double in size. When it is, turn out of the bowl, and knead for 2 more minutes.

Divide dough into 12 equal parts. Roll each into a long rope, and bring around to form a large open donut. Pinch ends together well.

Place on large greased cookie sheets, 6 to a sheet. Do not crowd.

Beat the egg with 1 tablespoon of water. Brush the top of each simit with egg and sprinkle liberally with sesame seeds.

Let rise until double, about 20 minutes. Bake in a preheated 350° oven for 20 minutes.

Remove from cookie sheets and cool on racks.

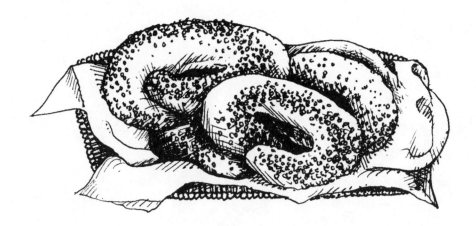

SWEETS AND DESSERTS

TURKISH SWEETS CAN BE DIVIDED into four general categories. First are the famous pastries, such as baklava. These are especially rich, and are not often served with a meal, but rather eaten with the afternoon tea or on special occasions.

The second group, the puddings, often conclude meals because they are considered somewhat lighter.

Turkish people believe that fruits are even a more fitting end to a meal, especially a meal that features a pilav; so cooked fruit desserts form a third category.

The last group are the special sweets, really candies, that are made for holidays, and as occasional treats.

Baklava

Of all Turkish sweets, baklava and its variations (mainly in shape) are most well known. Generations of bakers run shops that special-ize in their creation. It is a treat just to look at them neatly displayed in the bakery windows.

> ½ pound unsalted butter
> 1 pound phyllo sheets
> 2½ cups finely chopped, or coarsely ground walnuts
> 3 cups sugar
> 2 tablespoons lemon juice (½ lemon)
> 2 cups water

Melt the butter in a small saucepan. In a large oven pan (11 x 15 inches) lay out the first phyllo sheet. With a pastry brush, lightly coat with butter, add a second sheet and brush with more butter. Continue until ⅓ of the phyllo sheets are used.

Spread ½ of the nuts over the pastry, then continue buttering sheets of phyllo until ⅓ more is in the pan.

Spread the second ½ of the nuts over the pastry. Finish buttering and laying down sheets of pastry until the remaining ⅓ of the phyllo sheets are used up. Brush the top sheet with butter.

With a very sharp knife, cut through all the phyllo sheets to create 2 inch squares or diamond shapes. Pour any remaining butter over the top.

Bake uncovered in a preheated 250° oven for 1 hour, or until the pas-try is crisp and light golden.

In a small saucepan bring the sugar, lemon juice, and water to a boil. Reduce heat and simmer for 15 to 20 minutes. Allow to cool a bit, then pour over the baked baklava.

Allow all to cool at least 5 hours before serving.

Navels and Lips

This is a traditional pastry, served originally at Topkapi Palace. The same cake, soaked in syrup, takes two forms—hence the name.

Syrup:

>   3 cups sugar
>   3 cups water
>   1 tablespoon lemon juice

Pastries:

>   2 cups water
>   6 tablespoons butter
>   2½ cups flour
>   4 eggs
>   2 cups of vegetable oil for frying
>   1 cup heavy cream, whipped with 1 tablespoon
>   sugar

To make the syrup:

Bring the sugar, water and lemon juice to a boil. Lower the heat and simmer for 10 minutes. Cool.

To make the pastries:

Bring the water and butter to a boil. Add the flour all at once, and stir vigorously until it leaves the side of the pot in one smooth mass.

Remove from the heat. Add one egg at a time, beating vigorously with an electric mixer or by hand, until all eggs are incorporated. The dough should be thick, smooth, and shiny.

Divide dough in 2 pieces. One half will be "navels," and the other half will be "lips." To form navels, break off large, walnut-sized pieces.

Roll into a ball, then flatten into a 2½ inch circle and poke a finger through the middle. To form lips, start the same way, but fold the flattened circle in half to resemble lips. Use oil on your fingers if the dough sticks.

When all are formed, heat the oil to no more than 350°. Drop in a few lips and navels at a time. They will expand, don't crowd them. Fry slowly for about 10 minutes or until golden. Lower the heat if they are cooking in much less time, or the insides will be raw. Repeat until all are finished.

Drain each batch briefly on paper towels. Then soak them in the syrup for 10 minutes while the next batch is frying.

Place on a serving platter. When all are done, pour a little of the remaining syrup over top if you wish. Allow to cool.

Serve with a bit of whipped cream in the navel or between the lips. Makes 3 dozen.

Revani

This treat is a holiday or wedding dessert, but delicious any time. It is a dense sponge cake soaked in syrup.

Syrup:

        3 cups sugar
        4 cups water
        2 tablespoons fresh lemon juice (½ lemon)

Cake:

        9 eggs, separated
        ¾ cup sugar
        grated rind from 1 lemon
        2 cups semolina or farina (cream of wheat)
        ⅓ cup flour
        4 tablespoons unsalted butter, melted
        1 cup heavy cream, whipped with 1 tablespoon sugar
        ¼ cup ground nuts

To make the syrup: Bring sugar, water, and lemon juice to a boil, simmer 15 minutes. Cool.

To make the cake: Beat the egg yolks, sugar and lemon rind with an electric beater for 5 minutes or until pale yellow. Wash and dry the beater.

Fold the semolina and flour into the beaten yolks until well blended. Set aside.

Beat the egg whites with the clean beater until stiff. Alternate gently folding the egg whites and the melted butter into the yolk and flour mix.

Pour batter into a well greased and floured 9 x 12 inch or 10 x 12 inch baking pan. Bake in a preheated 350° oven for 40 minutes, or until a pick inserted in the center comes out clean.

Pour the syrup over the hot cake. Let it stand for several hours until the syrup is absorbed and the cake is cool.

Cut the cake into squares. Serve with whipped cream and sprinkle nuts on top.

Milk Pudding

Milk puddings like these are healthy and simple desserts. All kinds of ground nuts, coconut, or bits of dried fruit can be added.

> 2 tablespoons of cornstarch
> 2 tablespoons of rice flour
> 1 quart of whole milk
> ¾ cup sugar
> ¾ cup (total) of ground almonds, shredded coconut, pine nuts, pistachio nuts, raisins, or cut up dried apricots
> pinch of salt
> 1 teaspoon vanilla extract

Mix the cornstarch and rice flour in a small bowl with ½ cup water.

Pour the milk into a saucepan. Restir the cornstarch mix and add to the milk. Heat to a low boil, stirring constantly. Lower the heat.

Add sugar, your choice of nuts and fruit, and salt. Simmer and stir the mix for 20 minutes or until thickened. Add the vanilla extract during the last several minutes of cooking.

Turn out into one large or 6 individual oven proof serving dishes. Brown surface under a broiler. Refrigerate for several hours. Serves 6.

Citrus Pudding

A very light and refreshing dessert, it's easy to make, and perfect after a heavy meal.

> 5 level tablespoons cornstarch
> ½ cup lemon juice
> 1½ cups grapefruit juice
> 2 cups orange juice
> 1½ cups sugar
> 1 grapefruit, peeled and sectioned
> 2 oranges, peeled and sectioned
> 1 cup (total) of toasted coconut flakes, and chopped toasted almonds, hazelnuts, and pistachios
> 1 cup heavy cream, whipped with 1 tablespoon sugar

In a saucepan, combine the cornstarch, the three juices, and the sugar.

Bring to a boil, stirring constantly. Lower the heat, simmer and stir for 5 minutes.

Carefully stir in the grapefruit and orange sections. Simmer 2 more minutes. Stir in the assorted nuts and coconut.

Pour into individual dessert cups, or one large bowl.

Chill overnight. Serve with whipped cream. Serves 6 to 8.

Chicken Pudding

What appears to be an ordinary milk pudding has a surprise ingredient. This unusual dessert is sold in pudding shops throughout Turkey.

> 1 small whole chicken breast
> 7 cups whole milk
> 1½ cups sugar
> 4 level tablespoons cornstarch
> 9 level tablespoons of rice flour
> cinnamon

Boil the chicken breast in water for 15 minutes. Allow to cool, and remove all skin, bones, fat and tendons. Cut the breast into 1 inch squares. Carefully pull the meat into the tiniest possible threadlike shreds. You need 1½ cups of threads.

Rinse the shreds thoroughly in several changes of water and squeeze them dry.

In a large saucepan heat the milk and sugar.

Mix the cornstarch and rice flour in 1 cup water to dissolve. Slowly stir this mix into the hot milk, stirring constantly with a wire whisk.

Bring to a boil, lower heat to a simmer, stirring and cooking for 15 minutes.

Add chicken threads and mix well to completely incorporate them. Simmer over very low heat for 30 minutes, stirring every few minutes.

Pour into a 9 x 12 inch baking pan, let cool, cover, and refrigerate overnight. Sprinkle with cinnamon and cut into squares. Serves 10 to 12.

Pumpkin Hazelnut Compote

Especially in northern Turkey where the climate approximates north-ern coastal United States, pumpkins and pumpkin-like sweet winter squash are grown. Hazelnuts are also grown there, along the Black Sea. They combine well in this dessert.

1 4- to 6-pound pumpkin
2 cups of sugar
1 cup water
¾ cup chopped hazelnuts
1 cup heavy cream, whipped with 1 tablespoon
    sugar

Cut apart the pumpkin and remove the seeds. Peel the sections and cut into 1 inch cubes.

In a large mixing bowl, toss the sugar, water, and pumpkin pieces.

Transfer the pieces, plus all the water and sugar, to a baking pan. Cover tightly with foil and bake in a preheated 350° oven for 1 hour.

Check the water level after 30 or 40 minutes. Add more if necessary, or bake uncovered if it is too wet. There should be little water left and the pieces should be soft but not mushy.

Allow to cool, then refrigerate. Serve sprinkled with hazelnuts, and with the whipped cream.

Serves 6 to 8.

Poached Mixed Fruit

Ending a meal with cooked or fresh fruit is typically Turkish.

> 4 Granny Smith apples
> 4 large ripe peaches
> 1 tablespoon butter
> 40 to 50 whole cloves
> 2 cups sugar
> 1½ cups water
> ½ cup brandy (optional)
> 1 cup heavy cream, whipped with 1 tablespoon sugar

Wash and dry fruit. Cut each in half and remove seeds or pit.

Grease a baking pan with the butter, and in it place the fruit, side by side, skin side down. Push cloves into the top of the fruit, 2 or 3 per piece.

In a saucepan, mix the sugar with 1½ cups of water (or you may substitute up to ½ cup brandy for ½ cup of the water).

Bring to a boil to dissolve the sugar. Pour this syrup over the fruit, making sure that each depression contains some.

Cover and bake in a preheated 350° oven for 30 minutes. Uncover, spoon pan juices over the fruit, adding a bit more water if necessary.

Bake uncovered for 15 to 20 minutes more, or until the fruit is tender and the sugar is caramelized.

Allow to cool in the pan. Serve, one of each fruit to a plate, with the whipped cream. Serves 8.

Apricot Cream

Fresh and dried apricots are almost as popular as peaches in Turkey. Dried apricots are used very effectively in this nutritious dessert.

1 pound dried apricots
1 cup sugar
1½ cups water
Juice of 1 lemon
1 cup heavy cream, whipped with 1 tablespoon sugar
¼ cup chopped hazelnuts or almonds

Soak apricots in water overnight. Drain.

Combine sugar, water, and apricots in a saucepot. Bring to a boil, lower to a simmer, and cook uncovered very slowly for up to 1 hour. The water should be reduced to a syrup.

Add the lemon juice. Cook several minutes more. Remove from heat.

Chill for several hours. When ready to serve, gently fold in the stiffly whipped cream with the apricots. Spoon into individual bowls. Sprinkle nuts on top. Serves 6 to 8.

Helva

This helva tastes different and better than the store bought variety. It is usually served during religious holidays.

> 1 cup sugar
> 1 cup milk
> 1 cup water
> ½ cup butter
> 1 cup farina (cream of wheat)
> ½ cup pine nuts (pignolia)
> ¼ teaspoon cinnamon
> 1 cup heavy cream, whipped with 1 tablespoon
>   sugar

Bring the sugar, milk, and water to a boil. Lower the heat, and simmer for 15 minutes. Cool.

In a heavy pot, melt the butter and sauté the farina and the nuts until light brown. Do this slowly, over low heat for 20 minutes or more, stirring constantly. Be careful not to burn the farina.

Add the milk mix and the cinnamon to the sautéed nuts and farina, stirring constantly. Lower heat, stir and simmer until thick, about 5 minutes.

Remove from the heat, cover, and stir from time to time. After 10 minutes, turn into a lightly buttered mold. Chill overnight. Unmold, sprinkle with additional cinnamon. Slice thinly and serve with whipped cream. Serves 6 to 10.

Turkish Delight

Turkish Delight (or lokum) is sold in every confectioner's shop in Turkey, and is a popular holiday treat. You will need a candy thermometer to make it successfully.

4 cups sugar
3½ cups water
4 tablespoons lemon juice (1 lemon)
1 teaspoon cream of tartar
¾ cup cornstarch
1 drop red food coloring (optional)
¾ cup orange juice
1 cup coarsely chopped pistachio nuts
½ cup toasted coconut flakes
¾ cup confectioner's sugar

In a large saucepot, mix together the sugar, water and lemon. Bring to a boil, lower the heat, and gently simmer uncovered for 15 minutes.

Combine cream of tartar, cornstarch, red food coloring, and orange juice in a cup.

Slowly whisk it into the simmering sugar mix. Raise heat and stir often until a candy thermometer registers 235° to 240°. A drop in cold water should form a soft ball.

Remove from the heat, and stir in the nuts and coconut.

Pour into a greased 8 inch square cake pan. Chill. Cut into 1 inch squares with a sharp knife or scissors. Roll the squares in the sugar to coat. Let rest for a few hours. Roll in more sugar.

Cut 5 x 5 inch squares of wax paper. Roll each piece of candy tightly in paper, and twist the ends shut (like taffy). Store pieces in a covered container in the refrigerator.

Keeps well. Makes 5 dozen candies.

BEVERAGES

COFFEE, TEA, FRESH FRUIT DRINKS, yogurt drinks, and raki are popular throughout Turkey. The coffee is served in tiny cups, sweetened or unsweetened. It is thick and rich.

Tea is grown along the Black Sea, and delivering the small glasses of hot, sweetened tea to customers is the work of young boys in every city and town.

Everyone consumes refreshing pure fruit drinks. Fruit purées are strained, sweetened, and diluted with water—the forerunner of our sherbets.

Given the Turkish love of yogurt, it is not surprising that icy cold glasses of salted, diluted yogurt, called ayran, are served everywhere.

Moslems use very moderate (if any) amounts of alcohol, but one liqueur, raki, is considered a national drink. It is often mixed with water to create the so-called Lion's Milk that is consumed with assorted meze at a raki table.

Turkish Coffee

Select the best grade of roasted coffee, then have it ground to a very fine powder. Allow only ¼ cup of water for each serving.

> 1 cup water
> 2 tablespoons sugar, or less, to taste
> 4 heaping teaspoons coffee powder

Bring water, sugar, and coffee to a boil in a small pot. Remove from the heat, and divide the foam between 4 demitasse cups.

Return pot to the heat, and bring just to a boil again. Divide the coffee and grounds between the 4 cups.

Serve immediately. Serves 4.

Ayran

Ayran is considered a summer drink in Turkey because it is so refreshing.

> 2 cups yogurt
> 2 cups ice water
>   salt to taste

Beat or shake all the ingredients together. Refrigerate in a covered jar or pitcher. Serves 4.

Raki is a clear anise flavored liqueur which has its counterpart in Greece (ouzo), France (pernod), and Italy (anisette). It has the curious property of turning white in water, hence ...

Lion's Milk

1 ounce raki
5 ounces water
  ice cubes

Pour raki into a tall glass. Add water, ice, and stir. Serves 1.

Index